The Power of

Positive
Deviance

LEADERSHIP FOR THE COMMON GOOD

HARVARD BUSINESS PRESS

CENTER FOR PUBLIC LEADERSHIP
JOHN F. KENNEDY SCHOOL OF GOVERNMENT
HARVARD UNIVERSITY

The Leadership for the Common Good series represents a partnership between Harvard Business School Press and the Center for Public Leadership at Harvard University's Kennedy School. Books in the series aim to provoke conversations about the role of leaders in business, government, and society, to enrich leadership theory and enhance leadership practice, and to set the agenda for defining effective leadership in the future.

OTHER BOOKS IN THE SERIES

Changing Minds
by Howard Gardner

Predictable Surprises
by Max H. Bazerman and
Michael D. Watkins

Bad Leadership
by Barbara Kellerman

Many Unhappy Returns
by Charles O. Rossotti

Leading Through Conflict
by Mark Gerzon

Senior Leadership Teams
by Ruth Wageman,
Debra A. Nunes,
James A. Burruss, and
J. Richard Hackman

Five Minds for the Future
by Howard Gardner

The Leaders We Need
by Michael Maccoby

Through the Labyrinth
by Alice H. Eagly and
Linda L. Carli

*The Power of
Unreasonable People*
by John Elkington and
Pamela Hartigan

Followership
by Barbara Kellerman

Immunity to Change
by Robert Kegan and
Lisa Laskow Lahey

Crossing the Divide
edited by Todd L. Pittinsky

The Power of
Positive
Deviance

How Unlikely Innovators Solve the
World's Toughest Problems

Richard T. Pascale

Jerry Sternin

Monique Sternin

HARVARD BUSINESS PRESS

Boston, Massachusetts

11 10 9 8 7 6 5 4

Library of Congress Cataloging-in-Publication Data

Pascale, Richard T.
    The power of positive deviance : how unlikely innovators solve the world's toughest problems / Richard T. Pascale, Jerry Sternin, Monique Sternin.
        p. cm.
    ISBN 978-1-4221-1066-9 (hbk. : alk. paper) 1. Social problems. 2. Problem solving—Social aspects. 3. Diffusion of innovations. 4. Social change.
I. Sternin, Jerry. II. Sternin, Monique. III. Title.
    HN18.3.P37 2010
    362'.0425—dc22

                                                                    2009053370

The paper used in this publication meets the requirements of the American National Standard for Permanence of Paper for Publications and Documents in Libraries and Archives Z39.48-1992.

For Jerry

1938–2008

CONTENTS

Positive Deviance
and Health Care

Jerry Sternin was a professor of nutrition at Tufts University who, with his wife, Monique, had spent much of his career trying to reduce hunger and starvation in the world.* For a while, he was the director of a Save the Children program to reduce malnutrition in poor Vietnamese villages. The usual method was to bring in outside experts to analyze the situation and then to bring in food and implement agricultural techniques from elsewhere.

The program, however, had itself become starved—of money. It couldn't afford the usual approach. The Sternins had to find different solutions with the resources at hand.

So this is what they decided to do. They went to villages in trouble and got the villagers to help them identify who among them had the best-nourished children—who among them had demonstrated what Jerry Sternin termed a "positive deviance" from the norm. The villagers then visited those mothers at home to see exactly what they were doing.

*This foreword is adapted from Atul Gawande's commencement address given at the University of Chicago Medical School, June 2009.

Just that was revolutionary. The villagers discovered that there were well-nourished children among them, despite the poverty, and that those children's mothers were breaking with the locally accepted wisdom in all sorts of ways—feeding their children even when they had diarrhea; giving them several small feedings each day rather than one or two big ones; adding sweet-potato greens to the children's rice even though they were considered to be a low-class food. These ideas spread and took hold. The program measured the results and posted them in the villages for all to see. In two years, malnutrition dropped 65 to 85 percent in every village the Sternins had visited. Their program proved in fact *more* effective than those of the outside experts.

I tell you this story because we are now that village.

More than that, though, we in medicine have partly contributed to these troubles. Our country's health care is by far the most expensive in the world. It now consumes more than one of every six dollars we earn. The financial burden has damaged the global competitiveness of American businesses and bankrupted millions of families, even those with insurance. It's also devouring our government at every level—squeezing out investments in education, infrastructure, energy development, our future.

Like the malnourished villagers, we are in trouble. As President Obama has said, "The greatest threat to America's fiscal health is not Social Security, though that's a significant challenge. It's not the investments that we've made to rescue our economy during this crisis. By a wide margin, the biggest threat to our nation's balance sheet is the skyrocketing cost of health care. It's not even close." The public doesn't know what to do about it. The government doesn't know. The insurance companies don't know. There are health care experts who, during the course of the debate, have explained that a quarter of our higher costs are from having higher insurance administration costs than other countries and higher physician and nurse pay, too. The vast majority of extra spending, however, is for the tests, procedures, specialist visits, and treatments we order for our patients. More than anything, the evidence shows, we simply do more expensive stuff for patients than any other country in the world.

So the country is now coming to us who do this work in medicine. And they are asking us, How do they get these costs under control? What can they do to change things for the better?

Health care is not practiced the same way across the country. Annual Medicare spending varies by more than double, for instance—from less than $6,000 per person in some cities to more than $12,000 per person in others. I visited a place recently where Medicare spends more on health care than the average person earns.

You would expect some variation based on labor and living costs and the health of the population. But as you look between cities of similar circumstances—between places like McAllen and El Paso, Texas, just a few hundred miles apart—you will still find up to two-fold cost differences. A recent study of New York and Los Angeles hospitals found that even within cities, Medicare's costs for patients of identical life expectancy differ by as much as double, depending on which hospital and physicians they use.

Yet studies find that in high-cost places—where doctors order more frequent tests and procedures, more specialist visits, and more hospital admissions than the average—the patients do no better, whether measured in terms of survival, ability to function, or satisfaction with care. If anything, they seem to do worse.

Nothing in medicine is without risks, it turns out. Complications can arise from hospital stays, drugs, procedures, and tests, and when they are of marginal value, the harm can outweigh the benefit. To make matters worse, high-cost communities appear to do the low-cost, low-profit activities and services—like providing preventive-care measures, hospice for the dying, and ready access to a primary-care doctor—*less* consistently for their patients. The patients get more stuff, but not necessarily more of what they need.

Fixing this problem can feel dishearteningly complex. Across the country, we have to change skewed incentives that reward quantity over quality and reward narrowly specialized individuals instead of teams that make sure nothing falls between the cracks for patients and that resources are not misused. But how do we do it?

Let us think about this problem the way Jerry Sternin thought about that starving village in Vietnam. Let us look for the positive deviants.

This is an approach we're actually familiar with in medicine. In surgery, for instance, I know that there is more I can learn in mastering the operations I do. So what does a surgeon like me do? We look to those who are unusually successful—the positive deviants. We watch them operate and learn their tricks, the moves they make that we can take home.

Likewise, when it comes to medical costs and quality, we should look to our positive deviants. They are the low-cost, high-quality institutions like the Mayo Clinic; the Geisinger Health System in rural Pennsylvania; Intermountain Health Care in Salt Lake City. They are in low-cost, high-quality cities like Seattle, Washington; Durham, North Carolina; and Grand Junction, Colorado. Indeed, you can find positive deviants in pockets of most medical communities that are—right now—delivering higher value health care than everyone else.

We know too little about these positive deviants. We need an entire nationwide project to understand how they do what they do, how they make it possible to withstand incentives to either overtreat or undertreat, and spread those lessons elsewhere.

I have visited some of these places and met some of these doctors. And one of their lessons is that, although the solutions to our health-cost problems are hard, there *are* solutions. They lie in producing creative ways to ensure we serve our patients more than our revenues. And it seems that we in medicine are the ones who have to make this happen.

Here are some specifics I have observed. First, the positive deviants have found ways to resist the tendency built into every financial incentive in our system to see patients as a revenue stream. These are not the doctors who instruct their secretary to have patients calling with follow-up questions schedule an office visit because insurers don't pay for phone calls. These are not the doctors who direct patients to their side-business doing Botox injections for cash or to the imaging center that they own. They do not focus, the way businesspeople do, on maximizing their high-margin work and minimizing their low-margin work.

Yet the positive deviants do not seem to ignore the money, either. Many physicians do, and I think I am one of them. We try to remain oblivious to the thousands of dollars flowing through our prescription pens. There's nothing especially awful about that. We keep up with the latest technologies and medications in our specialty. We see our patients. We make our recommendations. We send out our bills. And, as long as the numbers come out all right at the end of each month, we put the money out of our minds. But we do not work to ensure that we and our local medical community are not overtreating or undertreating. We may be fine doctors. But we are not the positive deviants.

Instead, the positive deviants are the ones who pursue this work. And they seem to do so in small ways and large. They join with their colleagues to install electronic health records, look for ways to provide easier phone and e-mail access, or offer expanded hours. They hire an extra nurse to monitor diabetic patients more closely and to make sure that patients don't miss their mammograms and pap smears or their cancer follow-up. They think about how to create the local structures and incentives to make better, safer, more appropriate care possible.

Along the way, you will sometimes feel worn down, your cynicism taking over. But resist. Look for those in your community who are making health care better, safer, and less costly. Pay attention to them. Learn how they do it. And join with them.

—Atul Gawande

Atul Gawande is a general surgeon at the Brigham and Women's Hospital in Boston, staff writer for the *New Yorker*, and assistant professor at Harvard Medical School and the Harvard School of Public Health.

ACKNOWLEDGMENTS

This book is the product of twenty years of fieldwork, consulting, and teaching. It draws inspiration and insight from colleagues and clients, leaders of public and private organizations, community sponsors, and above all from those at the bottom of the pyramid. We have repeatedly witnessed how villagers and the uncelebrated members of governments, NGOs, and companies successfully tackle intractable problems when given an authentic opportunity to do so. We particularly acknowledge the many positive deviants (PDs) we have encountered on this journey— unknown and seemingly ordinary people whose innovative gifts, once discovered, have enabled entire communities to transform themselves.

Over the course of the three-year undertaking that has translated field experience to print, four individuals warrant special thanks: Ronald Heifetz for his meticulous critique of the manuscript and his formulation of adaptive change that lies at the heart of the PD approach; Lois Raimondo for her encouragement and editorial skills at a critical juncture in the journey; Jon Lloyd, who, in addition to pioneering the application of PD to health care, has been a steadfast partner in bringing this work to fruition; and Barbara Waugh, who summoned energy in the face of adversity to provide detailed editorial guidance and moral support.

Authors draw extensively on a bank account of goodwill among colleagues who invest countless hours reading and reviewing a work of this nature. Among these, we especially thank Don Baer, Denis Bourgeois, Lindy Brewster, Brownyn Fryer, Kalie Gold, Bradford and Maribeth Gowen, Martin Hermann, Lee Howell, Ashley Pascale, Keith Ruddle, and David Varney. We acknowledge our editor, Jeff Kehoe, who had a vision of what this book might be from the outset and doggedly raised the bar on the descriptive quality of the narrative.

A particular acknowledgment goes to Ann Carol Brown, who has endured the trials of the lead author over the three years and ten drafts that culminate in this published account. Her grace and emotional support are equaled by her intellectual contribution to the venture.

Our gratitude extends as well to the many PD facilitators who were key participants in the stories told and, as passionate members of the PD movement, continue to experiment and apply the PD approach to new frontiers. Among them: Mohammad Shafique and Amama Ambreen (Pakistan), Hien Nguyen (Vietnam), Paska Aber (Uganda), Susi Widiastuti (Indonesia), David Gasser (Mexico), Elina Debas (Argentina), Rajiv Jain, Cheryl Creen, Candace Cunningham, David Hares, Curt Lindberg, Mark Munger, and Margaret Toth (United States).

—Richard T. Pascale
  Pescadero, California

—Monique Sternin
  Concord, Massachusetts

ONE

Introduction

Against All Odds

IN THE AMAZON DELTA OF BRAZIL, cash crops now grow in tidal wetlands previously regarded as unsuitable for agriculture. Rosario Costa Cobral is a diminutive woman with determined eyes and prominent cheekbones. Her family occupies a small homestead on the banks of the great muddy river. With barely enough dry land to eke out a subsistence living, she sought a way to harness the vast swaths of rich delta soil inundated by twice-daily flooding. Rosario questioned the orthodoxy that farming and floodplains don't mix. A close observer of the Amazon's daily rhythms and seasonal cycles, she noted that in any given year the contours of the river bottom were relatively stable. Higher patches drained quickly when waters receded. Could plants survive if submerged only a few hours a day?[1]

Her first experiments were with cassava, a vigorous, water-tolerant staple of the Amazonian diet. Selecting for mutations within the species that flourished in especially wet places, she planted rootstock in the dry season when the river was low. Seedlings gained a sustainable foothold. Success emboldened her to experiment with other crops—lemons and chile peppers. Today, the family not only feeds itself but also generates an income, and Rosario is recognized by plant biologists and environmentalists for her pioneering discovery.

Looking at satellite photos taken of the Sahel Desert of Niger thirty years apart (1975 and 2005), one's attention is drawn to the anomaly of vast swaths of former desert that turned green. On closer examination, it's evident that vegetation is densest in the most densely populated regions. Most remarkable of all, this transformation took place in a fragile ecosystem where only 12 percent of the land is arable and 90 percent of the 13 million who reside there live off agriculture.[2] How, against impossible odds, did the community turn back the tide of sand dunes that had been inundating their huts?

Farmer Ibrahim Donjjimo had realized that the worsening trend was more than a seasonal aberration. The long-prevailing practice of clearing all trees to maximize crop density on scarce land had given rise to a treeless landscape. In the mid-1980s, Ibrahim began setting an example for other farmers in Guidan Bakoye by taking a counterintuitive step. Instead of clearing the saplings that sprouted from the earth each year, he protected them. In particular, he nurtured the indigenous gao and baobab trees, which flourish in harsh conditions. Turns out he stumbled on a highly effective, resource-neutral strategy. Fallen leaves add nutrients to the soil. Roots fix nitrogen from the air and help prevent erosion when infrequent, torrential rains batter the brick-hard earth. Because the deciduous trees are bare during the rainy season, canopy is absent when crops densely planted below their branches most need sun. Ibrahim's experiment bore fruit. After several years of observing Ibrahim's better crop yields and cash flow, a few began to follow suit. Then more. Today, farmers sell branches for firewood, sell or eat the fruit, and use the pods for animal fodder. Revenue from twenty trees brings $300 a year in additional income (a significant contribution to average per capita income). As tree planting spread from one town to another, the region began to evolve a more benign microclimate that mitigates the impact of searing droughts and arid winds.

These two stories of "positive deviants" share the common thread of *observable exceptions*. This is the unique point of entry for the positive deviance process: focus on the successful exceptions (i.e., positive deviants), not the failing norm. As a problem-solving process, this approach requires retraining ourselves to pay attention differently—awakening minds accustomed to overlooking outliers, and cultivating skepticism about the inevitable "that's just the way it is." Once this concept is grasped, attention to observable exceptions draws us naturally to the "who," the "what," and especially the "how."

Positive deviance? An awkward, oxymoronic term. The concept is simple: look for outliers who succeed against all odds.

This book comes from years of hearing "We've tried everything and nothing works." Positive deviance (PD) is founded on the premise that at least one person in a community, working with the same resources as everyone else, has already licked the problem that confounds others. This individual is an outlier in the statistical sense—an exception, someone whose outcome deviates in a positive way from the norm. In most cases this person does not know he or she is doing anything unusual. Yet once the unique solution is discovered and understood, it can be adopted by the wider community and transform many lives. From the PD perspective, *individual difference* is regarded as a community resource. Community engagement is essential to discovering noteworthy variants in their midst and adapting their practices and strategies.

Along a continuum of change tools, the positive deviance approach is one among a broad set of participatory methods. The basic premise is this: (1) Solutions to seemingly intractable problems already exist, (2) they have been discovered by members of the community itself, and (3) these innovators (individual positive deviants) have succeeded even though they share the same constraints and barriers as others.

The following chapters provide compelling evidence of a proven remedy for overcoming intractable problems. Its success in "impossible" situations demonstrates that we can make meaningful inroads against many of the seemingly insurmountable problems that confound the present and cast a shadow on our future (e.g., health care reform, tribal conflict, obesity, energy conservation). There is no shortage of places where PD could help.

Ours is a world of rising expectations: mass media allows anyone anywhere to evaluate his or her own material conditions relative to others. Against this backdrop of ubiquitous information on the comparative well-being of the many, there are glaring inequalities: 1.2 billion people live on less than $1 a day, 800 million do not have enough to eat, 170 million children are malnourished, and 3 million will die this year as a direct or indirect result of this condition.[3] Close to 20 percent of the world's population is functionally illiterate and lives under regimes that rank in the bottom quartile of nations with respect to human rights, rule of law, and representative government.[4] Approximately 27 million people are enslaved as the result of social bondage, onerous employment contracts, and human trafficking. India's close to 200 million Dalits (Untouchables) are not included in this number—yet many exist in a system of de facto bondage.[5] There is much to be done.

The PD Approach: Working Around the World

On December 14, 2008, the *New York Times Magazine* celebrated positive deviance as one of its annual "Year in Ideas" selections, devoting a full page and a half to the topic.[6] No ephemeral gimmick, clever rebranding of old ideas, or bogus claims of efficacy here. Piloted in Vietnam in 1990, proliferating at an exponential rate with diverse applications on all continents save Antarctica, the translation of this idea into practice has altered the lives of millions of people on the planet. Specifically, the process has been used in thirty-one nations in Africa, ten in Asia, five in Latin America, and in dozens of applications across the United States and Canada. Adaptations range from reducing gang violence in inner city schools in New Jersey and Pennsylvania to increasing the success rate of black entrepreneurs in South Africa; from providing access to markets across conflicted land on behalf of the Afar nomads of Ethiopia to improving smoking cessation among the 70 percent of inmates hooked on nicotine in the prisons of New South Wales; from reducing corruption in Kenya to improving the end-of-life experience and quality of death in Connecticut hospitals; from reducing the high dropout rates of minorities in California schools to the curtailment of sex trafficking of girls in Indonesia.[7] The Positive Deviance Initiative's Web site (www.positivedeviance.org) receives three thousand unique visitors each month.[8] Applications are growing exponentially.

Here are a few of the Positive Deviance Initiative success stories:

- A 65 to 80 percent reduction in childhood malnutrition in twenty-two Vietnamese provinces with a total population of 2.3 million.[9]

- A 30 to 50 percent reduction in childhood malnutrition in communities across forty-one countries worldwide.[10]

- A 30 to 62 percent reduction in transmissions of antibiotic resistant bacteria (MRSA) in three U.S. hospitals, and in the process, a bridging of the status divide in hospital hierarchies.[11]

- Dramatic reduction in neonatal mortality and morbidity in Pakistan, along with a blurring of defined gender roles and an increased voice for women.[12]

- A 50 percent increase in primary school student retention in participating schools in Misiones Province, Argentina, while reducing social
barriers between teachers and illiterate parents.[13]

- A 30 percent reduction in girl trafficking affecting nine hundred
children in poor villages in East Java by mobilizing all levels of the
community toward vigilance of girls at risk.[14] In one district with
reliable census data, thirty-three girls aged fourteen to seventeen
were trafficked in 2004. Four years later, as a direct result of the
Positive Deviance Initiative, that number had dropped to six. The
initiative has been expanded to one hundred communities in East
Java, encompassing 5,000 families and 19,500 at-risk children.[15]

- Thousands of female circumcisions (female genital mutilation, or
FGM) averted in Egypt over the last eight years, resulting in the
creation of dozens of FGM-free communities and a cadre of vocal
women's advocates.[16] Studies show a four percent drop in FGM
prevalence nationwide in the period from 1997 to 2000.

Deceptively Simple

The thirteenth-century Sufi mystic Nasrudin is a fixture of Middle
Eastern folklore. His parables combine wisdom with irony, logic with the
illogical, the superficial with the profound. In one, he is a notorious smug-
gler routinely crossing the frontier with his string of donkeys, saddle bags
loaded with straw. Customs inspectors search in vain for the contraband
that accounts for his steady accumulation of wealth. Years go by. Nasrudin
retires. One day he encounters the former chief of customs in a local tea
house. The retired official broaches a long-suppressed question:

"Nasrudin, as we are now old men who have ended our careers and are
no longer a threat to each other, tell me, during all those years, what were
you smuggling?"

Nasrudin replies: "Donkeys."

Invisible in plain sight. As will be seen in the chapters that follow, invisible positive deviants often "don't know what they know" (i.e., don't realize they are doing anything unusual or noteworthy). Living alongside peers, they flourish while others struggle. Also invisible in plain sight is the community's latent potential to self-organize, tap its own wisdom, and address problems long regarded with fatalistic acceptance. Once the community has discovered and leveraged existing solutions by drawing on its own resources, adaptive capacity extends beyond addressing the initial problem at hand, it enables those involved to take control of their destiny and address future challenges.

The pragmatic Mocua tribe of Mozambique have a succinct adage: "The faraway stick does not kill the snake." Positive deviants in your midst are the stick close at hand—readily accessible and successfully employed by people "just like us." No need for outside experts or best-practice remedies that "may work over there but won't work here." No need for deep systemic analysis or a resource-intensive assault on root causes. Just discover the closest stick and use it.

More Complicated Than Meets the Eye

The process seems straightforward: identify the PDs, discover their practices, and disseminate them to the broader community. Surely it can't be all that hard. Once a winning idea is discovered, common sense should do the rest. And there's the rub.

Harvard's Ronald Heifetz has made important contributions to our understanding of leadership and change—contributions that are directly relevant to PD methods. Heifetz's seminal insights begin with the distinction between formal and informal authority on the one hand, and leadership on the other.[17] As we will see, leadership can be an activity practiced without or beyond one's authority. He also provides us with the useful distinction between "technical" and "adaptive" work. Adaptive problems are embedded in social complexity, require behavior change, and are rife with unintended consequences. By way of contrast, technical problems (such as the polio virus) can be solved with a technical solution (the Salk vaccine) without having to disturb the underlying social structure, cultural norms, or behavior.

The PD process is a tool for adaptive work. Unfortunately, we are drawn instinctively to the "technical" stuff—the "what" (specific practices and tools that make the individual positive deviants successful). That's the easy part—and only 20 percent of the work. What matters far more is the "how"—the very particular journey that each community must engage in to mobilize itself, overcome resignation and fatalism, discover its latent wisdom, and put this wisdom into practice. This bears repeating: *the community must make the discovery itself*. It alone determines how change can be disseminated through the *practice* of new behavior—not through explanation or edict.

The configuration of this journey is decisive. The "leader" must blend into the landscape, adopting the natural contours of the social topography in which the journey takes place. The path taken creates the context for self-discovery and alters attitudes and behavior. Surprising things emerge.

The "How" and the "What"

The Altiplano of Bolivia rises a mile above the sea, a high plateau of searing emptiness and impoverished soil. Children of Ketchua Indian communities in this region suffer from high levels of stunting (short height for age). The invitation to conduct a positive deviance workshop seemed straightforward: mobilize the Ketchua to overcome stunting by identifying those not stunted, and discover what they are doing differently from everybody else.[18]

On one thing the NGO (nongovernmental organization) sponsors were clear: the PD inquiry would not find any nutritional practices of consequence. Experts (i.e., health specialists and nutritionists) had previously studied food consumption carefully. Their conclusion: everyone feeds their children exactly the same thing. Accordingly, and in the interest of expedience, they counseled that the focus should be on other causal determinants—exercise, hygiene, and so forth.

So the village mobilized itself to ferret out whatever was enabling some poor Ketchua families to have children of normal height when their neighbors did not.

Groups from the community visited homes of the not-stunted, looking for clues. Their stay included mealtime. They noted, just as expected, that each household cooked the same food in exactly the same large black kettles, hung over tripods, positioned over simple brick hearths. When asked what was in the pot, hosts' responses were identical: soup, composed of five or six carrots, eight to ten potatoes, one-quarter kilo of dried fish, and a local green leafy vegetable, shared by all family members.

The observers then watched as mothers served their children from the pot. A large ladle was used, and in every hut the child was given the same amount of soup poured into a tin cup of uniform size. The "experts" were vindicated, their prognosis reaffirmed. *"You see, everyone does eat the same food, and every child gets the same amount. That is our custom!"*

A relative from La Paz was a member of the group. Not as deeply embedded in the community (and thus not as programmed to "see" what others "knew"), she noted an important difference in a family whose children were not stunted: although the pot, cooking method, and contents of the broth were identical, the PD mother, using the same kind of ladle, served the soup differently. Instead of dipping off the top of the kettle, as was the common practice, she very deliberately scooped down to the bottom of the pot and ladled the child's bowl full of solids—carrots, potatoes, and fish. In traditional homes, conventional wisdom held that the ingredients in the bottom of the kettle were reserved for adults to fuel their daily labor. Possible nutritional consequences for early childhood development went unnoticed.

Awakened by spotting the novel in the familiar, the team's antennae were reset to more accurately see what they were observing. After visiting the other six PD families, local leaders, mothers, grandmothers, and Save the Children staff all agreed that they witnessed the same feeding of solids at all PD families. Uniformity surrounding the preparation of a broth of water, carrots, potatoes, fish, and greens (i.e., the *what*) distracted attention from one facet of the *how* (scooping from the bottom of the kettle and feeding the solids to the child) and its relationship to stunting. This behavior was embedded in long-standing tradition that determined the *why* and the how: only those engaged in daily labor warranted the additional sugars, starch, and protein. This was the difference that made the difference. Having confirmed the consequences of customs and ladling practices, the members designed a visiting program with other parents in the community. All witnessed the approach firsthand and observed that the children of these households were not stunted. Ensuing discussion changed the minds of many. Solids at the bottom of the kettle became a shared family resource.

When to Use the PD Approach

The positive deviance process is not suitable for everything. As noted earlier, it is unnecessary when a technical solution (e.g., drought-resistant corn; a vaccine for smallpox) exists. But the process excels over most alternatives when addressing problems that, to repeat, (1) are enmeshed in a complex social system, (2) require social and behavioral change, and (3) entail solutions that are rife with unforeseeable or unintended consequences. It provides a fresh alternative when problems are viewed as intractable (i.e., other solutions haven't worked). It redirects attention from "what's wrong" to "what's right"—observable exceptions that succeed against all odds.

It is also important that those in authority (e.g., village chiefs, funding NGOs, CEOs, etc.) be committed to giving the process a try. This often unfolds in a circuitous manner. Seldom do sponsors fully fathom what they are getting themselves into. (They often turn to PD as the remedy of last resort.) Over the course of the journey, they are changed in ways they did not foresee. Leaders and the led become intertwined in a cogenerative process in which all are altered. Outcomes are more often multiplicative than additive.

The Social System Is Key

The social fabric of each community has its own distinct pattern. This system holds intractable problems in place and must be unfrozen to allow new behaviors and mind-sets to evolve. The secret sauce of the PD process is how it engages and transforms the social dynamics that have kept things stuck. An analogy from behavioral biology makes the point:

In Britain in the late nineteenth century, certain birds gained notoriety for ingenuity displayed in pilfering cream from milk bottles. Underestimation of this wily species had the unintended consequence of cultivating its appetite for a convenient food source. Initially, dairymen delivered milk to the doorstep, dispensing it into customers' jugs. Cream floated to the top. Birds and other mammals gained unobstructed access to a tasty, high-protein dietary supplement. When, in 1894, caps were installed to thwart the raiders, the free lunch came to an abrupt end. Except, that is, for a few species of birds that figured out how to cope with the obstruction.

Pertinent to our story is *not* that a few clever individuals discovered that a well-placed peck could pierce the cap, but *how* the discovery was disseminated. The contrast between robins and magpies is instructive. Robins are highly territorial, live comparatively isolated lives, and vocalize primarily to demark their territory. The magpie, by way of contrast, is highly social and leverages its intelligence accordingly. Magpies, with a brain to overall body weight ratio only slightly lower than that of humans, exhibit unusual levels of social awareness. Rivaling chimpanzees, they can (along with humans, dolphins, elephants, and great apes) recognize their own unique image in a mirror. Concept of self is common to advanced social systems.[19]

Magpies are gregarious in winter, gather to roost at night, and collect in rooks as large as sixty-five thousand birds in mating season. They team up in bands to tease cats and dive-bomb predators. Demonstrating empathy and social altruism, cooperative breeding occurs from time to time, with additional adults helping to raise nestlings. Young magpies play elaborate social games, including king of the mountain, passing sticks, and sliding down smooth surfaces. They can work collectively to lift garbage bin lids as members take turns feeding. One flock figured out how to crack nuts by placing them in crosswalks, letting passing cars break the husks, and waiting for the red light before safely retrieving the contents. Unsurprisingly, the magpie's social intelligence disseminated bottle cap piercing techniques to millions of birds throughout Britain within a few years. The robin, on the other hand, was destined to compartmentalized success. Cap piercings by isolated individuals were not coupled with social diffusion. The occasional robin might pick up the technique from its mate. Juveniles might observe the method from a parent if the nest was within sight of a milk bottle. But absence of an evolved social network deprived the species as a whole.

Isolated positive deviants coexist in communities that operate like robins. A few may discover successful strategies to cope with difficult problems. But in the absence of a social process to disseminate innovation and incorporate it into the group repertoire, discovery bears few progeny.

The essential precondition to give learning the best chance is for the community to "discover" the answer for itself. If this essential work of self-discovery is outsourced to experts, the likely result is no pain, no gain. From the vantage point of the PD approach, the community must decide it has a problem serious enough to warrant collective attention, opt in to the activity of addressing it, enroll individual members to invest time and energy in the work of discovering the PDs and, later, disseminate discoveries through practice. As we shall see, these acts themselves transform the social system and behavioral change and learning take place. Paradoxically, while the PD process achieves all this by perturbing the social system, as compared to other approaches, it has the lowest perturbation to impact ratio. That's because it turns to solutions already proven *within* the system versus importing foreign solutions that arouse skepticism at best and outright sabotage at worst.

As will be noted throughout this book, PD works like nature works. (This isn't an analogy; it is the way it is.) Mutations in nature don't reinvent the whole genome of a species. Nature tinkers with a different shaped bird beak or slightly larger brain size that facilitates social intelligence. Natural selection does the rest, favoring variations that improve access to food and reproduction. Of course, in nature, this all plays out in evolutionary time scales of centuries or millennia. Employing identical principles, the PD process achieves this change within months or a few years.

Invisible Barriers

The greatest barrier to the application of the positive deviance approach comes not from the members of the community themselves but from the "experts" who seek to help them and from the authorities who preside over them. The reason traces to deeply ingrained views that those at the top of a hierarchy know more than those below, and that change is most efficiently driven top down and outside in. We call this the standard model.[20] Pervasive throughout the world, it is the primary means through which most people tackle change. Many leaders, field workers, facilitators, and consultants tend to identify gaps, devise initiatives to fill them, and create institutions dependent on top-down premises. Even when done with good intent, this approach may be largely ineffectual, insofar as it ignores a great big elephant in the room: social complexity.

In brief, the standard model entails top-down change in which (1) expertise is located near the top, (2) control of the implementation process is assumed, and (3) rollout is driven through the ranks. Default to the standard model is a conditioned reflex. It preserves the existing power and authority structure. Accordingly, a process such as positive deviance is often brushed aside as "too slow," "too problematic," "unnecessarily indirect and complex." People are assumed to be rational, and their social systems adaptable, and it is sufficient to "give them the answer and expect them to get on with it." Involving the community in a process of self-discovery? Letting people decide to opt in or opt out? Using practice (rather than knowledge or information) to disseminate new opportunities? All premises are widely discounted as "inefficient." Perhaps. But they are unbelievably effective.

As described in "The Standard Model at Genentech," biopharmaceutical pioneer Genentech did not want for "positive deviants." Its sales of a "miracle cure" for chronic asthma were twenty times higher than those of its peers. Yet the pervasive filter of the standard model largely diluted potential gains. Thus the conundrum: how could an enterprise as institutionally clever as Genentech so completely miss the golden opportunity within its grasp? More generally, why has the PD process, proven in forty countries as successful in tackling a wide variety of problems across a spectrum of organizations and social systems, had little or no uptake in for-profit companies? The answer: the standard model is so deeply socialized into companies that "it's just common sense." It acts like a lens that we see the world through. It distorts perception and limits choice without our knowing it.

The standard model is probably the best course of action for roughly 70 to 80 percent of change problems encountered. But when empirical experience leads us to conclude, "we've tried everything and nothing works," harnessing local understanding may be the only way to break the impasse.

The Standard Model at Genentech

In 2003, Genentech, the highly successful pioneer of genetically engineered drugs, introduced Xolair, a miracle cure for many chronic asthma sufferers.[a] Unlike standard treatments, which arrest asthma attacks after they occur, Xolair modulates the histamines in the immune system through periodic intravenous treatments in the doctor's office that address asthma preventatively. This allows the patient to lead a normal life, free of the fear of debilitating attacks. But despite Xolair's pharmacological superiority, sales remained well below expectations six months after launch.

As management wrestled to explain the disappointing results, analysts spotted an anomaly. Two otherwise ordinary salespeople among a national force of 242 were selling twenty times more Xolair than their peers. Here were classic positive deviants. Two women responsible for the Dallas and Fort Worth territories had successfully overcome resistance within the medical community and gained extraordinarily high rates of acceptance.

Investigation shed light on the breakthrough. Genentech's stronghold is cancer medicine. The clientele for its mainstream products—oncologists and pulmonary specialists—routinely administer chemotherapy, an infusion procedure performed in doctors' offices on an outpatient basis. Xolair's market, in contrast, is allergists and pediatricians—the primary source of care for asthma patients. Infusion protocols (delivering medication in the form of an IV drip) require infusion rooms, infusion couches, and infusion nurses. This is unfamiliar territory for allergists, pediatricians, and their nursing staffs.

The positive deviants from the Dallas and Fort Worth area grasped this stumbling block. Product acceptance could not be achieved through the standard information exchange between the Genentech rep and the physician on a routine sales call (i.e., more convincing data demonstrating Xolair's pharmacological superiority was beside the point). The real obstacles were the doctors' fear of seemingly exotic procedures, concerns about time-consuming insurance approvals, and worries that patients would be exposed to unnecessary risks. The crux of the matter was mind-set and behavior. The challenge, therefore, was to expand the doctors' repertoire and transform the office culture.

So the salespeople redefined their role as on-the-court consultants, guiding doctors and nurses through the process of readying Xolair for infusion and administering it to patients. They taught administrators how to negotiate the labyrinth of paperwork to secure reimbursement from insurance companies. They pitched the drug's beneficial lifestyle impacts for the patients for whom it had received FDA approval (e.g., they could now own pets and participate in outdoor sports). Instead of applying force against force (i.e., overcoming resistance with persuasion), they used judo by engaging the doctors' teams in enlarging their practice repertoire and enriching the job content of nurses and administrators. They had discovered what armies of Genentech's market researchers had missed. They were successful because they had morphed from salespeople into change agents.

Our narrative seems destined for an upbeat ending. What actually unfolded testifies to both the persistence and perversity of the standard (top-down) model. Genentech prescribed a top-down protocol for its sales force that relied on data that demonstrated Xolair's superiority. The aberrant sales results evoked consternation and scrutiny because they did not adhere to this orthodoxy. Management's initial assumption was that the sales team was "cheating"—poaching other territories or shortcutting safeguards, somehow encouraging the drug's use for age groups not authorized by the FDA, or overstocking doctors' drug inventories with a product with a short shelf life. Only when an external market research firm confirmed that the true source of success was the company's innovative employees (who were not violating ethical or procedural rules) did management consider the merits of their consultative strategy. But trusting in the power of "disseminated information" and cascading intention, they implemented a conventional best-practices rollout. Management insulated the two successful reps from their peers by doing the fact finding themselves. (The "positive deviants" debriefed their bosses on a conference call.) Next, management composed a broadcast e-mail followed up by a conference call directing other reps to consider a consultative approach to increase sales of Xolair. Result? Lukewarm acceptance and modest improvement in market penetration.

a. Richard Pascale interviews with Genentech, March 9, 2004; members of Xolair sales force and management teams (including Martin Babler), March 9, 2004; and Bob Mackey, May 18, 2005.

The following chapters present in-depth narratives illustrating the power of positive deviance in alleviating some of the world's toughest problems. Written in the voice of respective coauthors, these stories trace the evolution of the positive deviance process from its inception in Southeast Asia to the present. Jerry tackles malnutrition in Vietnam; Monique broaches the undiscussable issue of female genital circumcision in Egypt and the daunting cultural issues affecting infant mortality in the North-West Frontier Province of Pakistan. Jerry describes how the approach was used to address the life-threatening epidemic of antibiotic-resistant bacteria in the complex setting of Veterans Administration hospitals. Richard provides an account of the highly successful (but circumscribed) attempts to apply PD in corporate settings and the challenges faced in Uganda of overcoming misconceptions about the positive deviance process that arise from learning about it in a book.

TWO

Childhood Malnutrition in Vietnam

From Peril to Possibility

The Chinese character for the word crisis *is composed of two ideograms: one is most closely translated as "imminent peril"; the second reflects the idea that new possibilities lurk in the shadow of uncertainty. Nothing better captures the circumstances that greeted Jerry and Monique when they arrived in Vietnam. Jerry provides the following account.*

V IETNAM RECEIVED SUBSIDIZED RICE imports from its allies during the war. These shipments masked wartime disruptions and the low productivity of its collective farms. Following the war, a border dispute with China and deterioration of the Soviet economy brought an abrupt end to this source of relief. In the late eighties, by government decree, Vietnam's collective farms were privatized, each family allocated a small parcel of land. Disruption to cereal production was staggering. The health care system also began to collapse under the weight of parallel shifts to privatization. By 1990, about 65 percent of all Vietnamese children under the age of five suffered from malnutrition.

Born in 1986, Kim-Mai had the rosy cheeks and cherubic face of a Vietnamese doll. She was the youngest of three siblings and the daughter of a very poor family. Precocious for her age, she chattered incessantly and delighted in the small discoveries of daily life that grown-ups find mundane. Grandparents on both sides had perished during the war. Her father suffered from chronic pain after a bicycle accident. When the government decided to distribute the land among the farmers, she could not comprehend the implications. But she was soon to experience them firsthand.

When the hard times began, her family could not keep up with the spirit-sapping toil of rice farming. Harvests were meager. She began to go hungry—always hungry. When occasional relief supplies arrived, family members would gorge themselves to the last calorie.

Undernutrition can manifest itself in two ways: acute (which arises from short-term inadequate food intake) and chronic (proceeding from the lack of adequate nutrients over a longer period of time). Both lower resistance to infection due to weakened immune systems and vitamin deficiencies. Both cause children to waste away. Chronic undernutrition causes irreparable stunting—survivors suffer from mental and physical impairment. One in five perish.

Kim-Mai was typical of many malnourished children in the Vietnamese countryside. Initially, access to calories kept her "full" but inadequately nourished. Lacking sufficient protein and vitamin intake, she became lethargic. As her digestive system slowed down, liquid collected in her stomach and her belly became distended. Her feet began to swell. Touching the tops of her feet left an imprint as if her skin were Play-Doh. Her black hair began to turn red.

Kim-Mai was unlucky. The following year's harvest was even worse—insufficient to feed her brothers and parents. And she was a girl, which translates into getting the leftovers. *Chronic* malnutrition set in as the calories, protein, and carbohydrates available were simply insufficient to fuel her physiological engine. Her once attractive mane of shiny black hair thinned considerably. Kim-Mai's body was husbanding its meager reserves to keep her heart pumping, lungs breathing, and other vital organs from shutting down.

As lethargy set in, Kim-Mai became inactive. A once curious child, she now followed moving objects with her eyes but not her head. Susceptibility to disease increased. Diarrhea, endemic in the villages, accelerated Kim-Mai's dehydration and further impaired digestion. Urination dwindled. As flesh lost its elasticity and acquired the texture of dry parchment, she withered and appeared very old. Formerly endearing facial features were receding toward the foundational skull. Disproportionately large eyes peered out from cavernous sockets.

In 1990, the U.S. NGO Save the Children (SC) received an unprecedented invitation from the government of Vietnam to create a program that would enable poor villages to solve the all-pervasive problem of childhood malnutrition. Ironically, the invitation was extended during the period of the U.S. government's trade embargo against Vietnam, which sought to enforce the Paris Peace Accords through economic sanctions.

Save the Children asked me if I would leave my post as director of their Philippines program and go to Vietnam to open a program there. Although (or because!) the challenge was so formidable, I eagerly accepted, and in December 1990, Monique, our son Sam (who had just turned ten), and I left for Hanoi to become the thirteenth, fourteenth, and fifteenth Americans to take up residence in that city. We were met at the airport by our handler and translator, Ms. Hien—her severe face uncompromised by makeup, inquisitive brown eyes framed by large horn-rimmed glasses, thin lips, obsidian black hair cropped squarely above the shoulder, gray Mao suit with smartly creased slacks, and sturdy low-heeled oxfords. She introduced herself with few pleasantries. "You're the Sternins? Follow me." Bundling our belongings into a black Russian Volga, we threaded our way through the obstacle course of traffic along Hanoi's main north/south artery: human-drawn carts, pedicabs, bicyclists balancing awkward loads on the ends of bamboo poles resting across padded shoulders—wire baskets stacked high with shimmering red tomatoes, cumbersome clusters of delicate yellow bananas, five-gallon jerry cans of gasoline, chickens squawking in protest at being transported upside down. One cyclist was shouldering a rattan sofa while maneuvering through the vehicular chaos. An hour later we were deposited at our tiny quarters in Hanoi.

The government knew that something needed to be done. While a traditional supplemental feeding program from local and international relief agencies provided temporary solutions, they were economically unsustainable. Although there were significant gains in children's nutritional status during the period of program implementation, they were all but lost after the programs ended.

The reasons for the failure were not difficult to discern: villagers were passive program beneficiaries, neither encouraged nor required to change any of the underlying practices that had led to their children's malnutrition, or even see that these practices could be playing a part. The nutritional gains realized during program implementation were completely based on external food resources. These were no longer accessible to villagers after the implementing agency departed. Further, the major focus of traditional nutrition programs was on providing additional food, with little or no attention paid to improving the all-important child care, hygiene, and health-seeking behaviors associated with good nutritional status. In short, "they came, they fed, they left," and nothing changed.

The daunting challenges facing us, I quickly learned, were not just physical and programmatic; there were political hurdles as well. Many officials were not at all happy to have Save the Children, an American NGO, working in Vietnam at the very time the U.S. government was actively trying to bring the country into line through its economic embargo. The depths of those convictions were made clear when I was summoned to the Ministry of Foreign Affairs the week after our arrival. Mr. Nhu, a high-ranking official, greeted me in his spartan, hospital-green office and offered me the folding chair next to his desk. He was eager for me to know that he personally was very supportive of Save the Children and had been instrumental in inviting us to come to Vietnam. After a few perfunctory pleasantries, he got straight to the point. "Sternin, there are many officials who do not want you in this country," he warned. "You have six months to demonstrate impact, or I'm afraid my ministry will be unable to extend your visa."

Six months! An adrenalin rush. As a veteran in this line of work, I knew it usually takes a year just to begin to set up an office in a new country. Staff has to be identified and trained, office space secured, potential development partners identified, meetings held with potential program communities, and so forth. Here we were, being asked to actually demonstrate program impact within six months. I was stunned by the enormity of the challenge and only minimally reassured by my conviction that great opportunities are often accompanied by great risk. But there it was: a very real danger of failure given only six months to show impact. Juxtaposed to this was the extraordinary opportunity if we could somehow succeed.

Some issues were clear. The government of Vietnam simply didn't have the resources to address the problem of ongoing malnutrition in ten thousand rural villages. A strategy had to be identified to enable the villagers to somehow solve the problem themselves. The focus clearly had to be preventive as well as curative. Given our six-month deadline, and my conviction that any solution must be sustainable, I knew that this couldn't be "business as usual." We would have to find a new approach based on something that was already working using resources already available. These defining criteria all pointed toward an obscure research construct: positive deviance (PD).

Although the PD concept had been around for many years, it had simply been used to describe those statistical outliers encountered in fieldwork who outperform the norm. In 1989 Marian Zeitlin and her colleagues at the Tufts University School of Nutrition published a collection of studies from around the world that identified well-nourished children from poor families (and labeled them *positive deviants*).[1] The children were somehow thriving in vulnerable populations with severe nutritional constraints. Zeitlin identified factors that led the positive deviants to better outcomes than others in their community. The findings ended there: case studies of field aberrations. She did not take the final step of suggesting an approach that might harness these positive deviant strategies to achieve nutritional gains. But the idea intrigued me. If some individuals in a community were better able to solve problems than others with access to exactly the same resources, could we use that provocative discrepancy? With five months left until our visa deadline, necessity became the mother of experimentation.

Monique and I turned to Ms. Hien, who had warmed to us over those first uncertain weeks. She would become a confidante and advisor on all matters of culture, politics, survival, and our closest friend in Vietnam. Born in 1959, Hien had lived through the horrors of the American war. She had a keen intellect (several years later she would attend the Kennedy School at Harvard on a full scholarship) and a whimsical sense of humor that magically crossed our cultural divide. Hien got my jokes and even laughed at them.

Hien set up a meeting for the three of us with Hanoi-based Health Ministry and People's Committee officials to discuss potential pilot sites. They identified several possibilities. We finally chose Quang Xuong District in Thanh Hoa Province, a torturous four-hour ride south of Hanoi. It was a particularly poor area with extremely high malnutrition rates. We were eager to choose a location relatively close to the capital. If successful, the pilot site could be easily reached by government officials and other visitors, making it easier for us to scale up the demonstration program. (In retrospect, I reflect on how naively optimistic our concerns with "scaling up" were, given that we didn't have a clue whether PD would even work.)

In late January 1991, with only twenty weeks left until the impact-or-no-visa deadline, our gang of three rented an oxidized black sedan of mixed Soviet parentage. A mechanic, perhaps thwarted by exigencies of the war and deprived of his true calling as a surgeon, had transplanted a tractor engine to power the beast—a loud, tireless, fume-spewing diesel. Shock absorbers designed for trucks reliably communicated every pothole to the spine. The vehicle's interior made few concessions to creature comforts. The simple act of cranking the passenger window up and down exacted as much effort as operating the tire jack. We made the first of what would be hundreds of visits from Hanoi to Quang Xuong in this car. The seventy-five-mile, four-hour journey south on Highway 1 crossed three bridges, one a train trestle (shared alternately by the decrepit Hanoi-Saigon steam locomotive, all motorized traffic, and scores of market-bound bicycles).

Over the next week we met with members of the People's Committee, Women's Union, and Provincial Health Cadre to discuss the proposed project. We emphasized our commitment to collaborating with villagers to identify from within solutions to the problem of malnutrition. The independent and proud Vietnamese officials, all of whom had suffered greatly during the "American War," warmed to the idea that solutions would be Vietnamese rather than foreign and that the project would not cause dependency. They were also clearly skeptical that it would work.

My most important and difficult meeting turned out to be with the deputy chairman of the People's Committee of Thanh Hoa Province, Mr. Bhu. The meeting was set for early afternoon, and I spent all morning rehearsing my short introduction to our proposed PD program in Vietnamese. If I could dazzle my host on our first encounter with my command of the language, we would be off to a great start.

When I arrived at the People's Committee provincial headquarters, Mr. Bhu invited me into his office, where he was still in chambers with several chain-smoking local cadres. I had expected a private meeting and was somewhat thrown by the smoke-filled room and all the quizzical faces around the table. I put aside my prepared speech for a moment to apologize for my interruption of their ongoing meeting. "I won't spend too much time talking with you as I know you are all very busy," I said. A look of utter disbelief and tentative outrage on every face in the room. A long moment of excruciating silence—then gales of laughter from Bhu and his fellow officers. Vietnamese is a tonal language. Choose the wrong tone and you are in deep trouble. Instead of saying *bận* (busy) with a level tone, I had used a falling tone (*bản*). The result: my opening salutation was, "I won't spend too much time talking with you as I know you are all very dirty!" So much for my dazzling entry!

Mr. Bhu spent little time on the traditional Vietnamese formalities and got right to the point: "How much money and what kind of material inputs are you going to provide?" I explained that to create a sustainable model, most of the inputs would have to come from the villagers themselves. We would, of course, provide some material input, but would focus attention on training and developing the capacity of the villagers to address their own problems. Responsible for development of an extremely resource-poor province, he reluctantly gave the go-ahead. But it was clear to me that he wasn't at all pleased with the rich American NGO that promised nothing more than "capacity building" and "self-reliance" instead of medical equipment and supplemental food—in his mind, the stuff of real assistance.

We began immediately to conduct a sample nutritional baseline survey of children in four villages proposed by Mr. Bhu as potential pilot sites. The good news was that the villages definitely needed help and provided a perfect opportunity for the first PD trial. The bad news was that 63 percent of the children under the age of three were malnourished. (The vast majority of the well nourished were members of comparatively well-to-do families or had access to special resources, such as a rich uncle in a neighboring hamlet.)

Immediately after the sample survey, we met with the village leaders and members of all the established community networks (the local People's Committee, Women's Union and Farmer's Union, and community health cadres) to discuss the proposed project in each of the four villages or "communes." It was the first time these stakeholders had met to discuss children's health. Surprisingly, we found our work (there and elsewhere in the world) was often a catalyst for community collaboration. Villagers shared their beliefs about the causes of malnutrition and talked about their hopes for the future. We explained our desire to help the community permanently solve their malnutrition problem. Fortunately, the villages had previously had supplementary food programs initiated by the World Food Program, a UN agency. Their experience provided a great backdrop against which to explain and contrast the positive deviance approach:

Hien: Have you ever had a supplementary feeding program here before?

Villagers: Yes.

Hien: What was the result of the program?

Villagers: Our children got healthier and put on weight.

Hien: What happened after the program was over?

Villagers: Our children became malnourished again.

Hien: Why?

Villagers: Because when the project was over there was no one to give us those foods (oil, milk powder, high-protein biscuits) which made our children better.

Hien: Well then, what would you like to see different in the future?

Villagers: We want to see our children get better, and stay better.

Hien: Do you think it would be better if you could do that on your own, rather than be dependent on outside help?

Villagers: Of course, but how is that possible? We are a poor village.

Armed with faith rather than actual proof, I explained that the PD approach might help them address the problem of malnutrition through the identification of solutions that already existed within their community. They would require some initial help with those children who were already malnourished (we planned to supplement their diets with eggs or tofu), but the PD approach could show them how to independently sustain their children's improved nutritional status once they had been rehabilitated. If this was going to work, however, the villagers would have to assume major responsibility for the initiative.

First Steps: Baseline and Common Practices

Is blue different? Silly question. Only by knowing the context—different from what—is it possible to differentiate PD practices from the norm. Until we determine *what* everybody is doing *today*, we can't spot the exceptional and successful strategies. This turns out to be the most rigorous part of the PD process. The baseline establishes a base of facts from which progress can be assessed. This means collecting empirical data to document the current condition (e.g., weighing children), agreeing on criteria for inclusion (to ensure that potential positive deviants won't be confused with individuals who aren't at risk or have access to special resources—e.g., a very poor person subsidized by a relative), and then cataloging common practices.

The first step toward all this was the creation of Village Health Committees (VHCs), composed of volunteers from the Women's Union, Farmer's Union, People's Committee, and the village health cadre. These volunteers from among the ranks would become the shepherds of the yet-to-be-determined process. Although we weren't consciously trying to establish any PD guidelines at the time, we were discovering that the best people to manage a program aren't those who are appointed by the powers that be, but those who are passionate enough about the mission to self-select.

The self-selected health volunteers were eager to get started. Assisted by local health staff and village leaders, they then began by weighing the children and charting their nutritional status by placing a dot on a simple card with two axes—one for age and the other for weight. The weighing device was a handheld fulcrum used for weighing rice, with a bucket for the child on one end of the weighing bar and weights on the other. Some children had previously been weighed during the sample nutritional baseline survey (the health volunteers conducted a community-wide growth-monitoring campaign in late February 1991). But this was the first universal weighing of all children under three in these communities. After the children had been weighed, we met with the health volunteers and the village leadership to review the findings. Consistent with the pattern of the earlier sample survey, 64 percent (rather than 63 percent) of the children suffered from some degree of malnutrition.

Because we sought solutions to the problem of malnutrition that would be accessible to everyone in the community, particularly to the most vulnerable, we asked the volunteers to do a socioeconomic ranking of all households in their hamlet. With no preset categories, the volunteers chose "poor," "very poor," and "very, very poor" as accurate descriptors of the economic status of almost all village families.

When they completed their rankings, we gathered the volunteers beneath the corrugated tin roof of the commune's town hall. Stout timbers at each corner supported this modest unwalled structure. Makeshift benches were arranged on the earthen floor. A blackened panel of plywood served as a writing surface and soft stone as chalk. As expected, two-thirds of the children were malnourished.

Time for the Somersault

Simple idea, really. The "somersault question" draws on the concept of inversion. It turns circular logic on its head by looking at an issue the other way around. (Akin to the adage: "The chicken is the egg's way of reproducing itself.") All that was required was *mirroring back* the sweeping generalizations regarding village malnutrition. The common explanation of the cause of malnutrition was poverty. We asked the volunteers if any of the well-nourished children came from "very, very poor" families. They looked at the tally. Several literally rose in excitement: "Có, có vài cháu rất nghèo nhưng không bị suy dinh dưỡng!" (Yes, yes, there are some children from very, very poor families who are well nourished!) "Do you mean," we asked, "that it's possible today for a very, very poor child in this village to be well nourished?" "Có, có!" came the reply. "It is, it is!"

The "Có, có!" epiphany on that defining day in February represents an indelible milestone in a career devoted to community change. It was clear that the discovery of a possible way forward by those who needed to believe that one already existed quite literally triggered an attitudinal somersault. The "aha" moment broke the fundamental assumption of experts and residents alike that "villages are poor and have no solutions." Allowing the villagers to discover there were exceptions among them created the context for investigating what was going on. As the positive deviance approach became refined over the following months and years, the Vietnamese "Có, có" equivalent of the "aha" moment took on ever-increasing importance. It has become a centerpiece of the PD design.

Having established the possibility of being well nourished despite extreme poverty, the volunteers explored the implications of the discovery. If some very poor families in the village had well-nourished children, it might be possible for their poor neighbors to have well-nourished children as well. This realization set the stage for what would become the inquiry phase of the approach: a process that identifies how some members of a community, faced with the same constraints as their neighbors and with access to no special resources, are uniquely able to avoid or overcome a pervasive problem.

Because positive deviants are deviant only within the context of their divergence from the norm (in this case, the traditional feeding, caring, and sanitation behaviors), we needed to identify common practices and behaviors before we could distinguish what the positive deviants were doing that was different. Over the next week, the trained volunteers conducted many focus group discussions in each of the villages. Meeting informally with mothers, grandmothers, fathers, older siblings, and community health providers, they discussed conventional practices regarding feeding, caring, and sanitation.

One of the insights that emerged was the importance of learning through contrast. For many, the first reaction to PD is often, "Oh yeah, we do that, I know that." This dismissive acknowledgement overlooks important details and differences. What is most difficult to grasp when presented with a new idea is not what about the idea is similar, but what is *different*. Identifying PD behaviors without looking first at how they contrast with the norm would be a much less powerful provocation for change.

When Is "Enough"?

After the first eight conversations, the Vietnamese volunteers reported that they were hearing the same information over and over again and weren't learning anything new or useful. We were about to call a halt to the effort when one of the volunteers registered a cautionary note. Tuyen, a mother of three and one of the most active volunteers, explained, "Although I'm not learning anything new either, there are still another three or four households in my hamlet that haven't participated in these focus groups. Several of them are the poorest people in the hamlet. If I don't go and listen to them, they will feel hurt, and conclude that I don't think they have anything to contribute. If I'm going to need their cooperation later on when we begin our program, I better go and listen to their ideas."

Once it was articulated, all grasped the importance of Tuyen's insight. The value of the group conversations was not merely extracting useful information from a wide variety of stakeholders, but also listening to their ideas and beliefs and inviting them to be an integral part of the creation of the program. Ever since, one of the first steps in the PD process, whether applied in villages in the developing world or hospitals in the United States, has been for the local facilitators to listen to as many people in their community as possible, irrespective of the added value to the listener's learning curve. This engenders the broadest ownership.

Within a few weeks, we completed the focus groups and had a firm grasp of the common practices that impacted kids' nutritional status in the four villages. The health volunteers had held back visiting the very poor families with well-nourished children. Now the challenge was to see if we could actually identify some uncommon practices that would account for these kids' superior nutritional status.

Hien, several health volunteers, and a few village leaders divided into teams and went out to see if our PD hypothesis would actually work. Over a two-day period we visited six households, asked questions, and most importantly, observed how moms and other family members fed and cared for their PD kids. We had arranged to visit the PD homes an hour or so before mealtime so that we could observe, rather than merely ask about, the actual food preparation and hygiene. In every case, our real-time presence during food preparation, cooking, and serving proved to be invaluable.

Uncommon Practices

What the PD caretakers reported doing and what they actually did was often at odds. This wasn't the result of their being disingenuous, but rather of their not being conscious of all their actual practices (i.e., of the invisible not yet visible). One of the PD moms, for example, said that she only washed her daughter's hands just before eating. But the team present during the mealtime noted that in addition to the initial washing, the mom washed the little girl's hands again after she had petted a dog that had strayed into the house while she was eating, and then a third time when she started playing with her brother's muddy flip-flops.

An interview *without actual observation* with this PD mom would have reported that she (like many others in the village) "washed her child's hands before the meal"—not uncommon. On-site observation, however, allowed for the discovery that the mom washed her child's hands every time they came in contact with anything unclean throughout the entire process of eating (an uncommon PD practice). Situational learning has become a core component of the PD inquiry in all settings and has captured many of the most useful *hows*, not just the *whats*.

After visiting the positive deviants' homes, we reassembled at the community meeting hall. There was a palpable buzz in the air. Each team had discovered several uncommon behaviors among the PD families. First and foremost, in every instance where a poor family had a well-nourished child, the mother or father was collecting tiny shrimps or crabs (the size of one joint of one finger) from the rice paddies and adding these to the child's diet along with the greens from sweet potato tops. Although readily available and free for the taking, conventional wisdom held these foods to be inappropriate, or even dangerous, for young children.

Along with the dietary addition of shrimps, crabs, and greens and the atypically strict hand hygiene in five of the six PD households, other positive deviant practices emerged. These involved frequency and method of feeding, quality of care, and sanitation. For example, most families fed their young children only twice a day, before parents headed to the rice fields early in the morning and in the late afternoon, after their return. Because children under three years of age have small stomachs, the youngest children could eat only a small percentage of the available rice at each sitting. PD families, however, instructed the caregiver (an older sibling, a grandparent, or a neighbor) to feed these children regularly. Their kids were fed four or even five times a day. Result: using exactly the same amount of rice spread out over an additional two or three meals, the PD kids were getting twice the calories as their neighbors who had access to exactly the same resource. This was the first of countless examples illustrating that PD practices often reflect not only *what* is being done differently, but *how* it is being done.

The Magic of Doing

Through the PD inquiries, community members had discovered for themselves what it took for a very poor family to have a well-nourished child. The challenge now was to get people to translate that knowledge into practice. We convened a meeting with the volunteers, local leaders, and health clinic staff to get their input. The aim was to design a process to "teach" villagers the special practices that had been discovered.

Lots of ideas for education sessions, hamlet meetings, and attention-getting posters were offered. Everyone was excited by what we had "learned" and the natural instinct was to "tell" others about it. Then, as the meeting came to a close and the crowd was dispersing, something occurred that might easily have been lost in the general distraction of the moment. One of the older volunteers observed loudly enough for others to hear: "Một nghìn nghê không bằng một xêm, một nghìn xêm không bằng một làm" (a thousand hearings aren't worth one seeing, and a thousand seeings aren't worth one doing). Then, goodbyes all around. "Hẹn gặp lại!" "See you again next week."

As we made our way back to the car (now sardonically referred to as "the beast") for the long ride back to Hanoi, Hien, Monique, and I shared that eerie feeling that something subliminal had just flashed by and we needed to grasp it. "*Seeing trumps hearing, but doing trumps seeing!*" All the way back to Hanoi (which took seven rather than the usual four hours that evening because a train had broken down on the bridge), there was an elusive something that kept clawing for attention.

Perhaps because we were held captive by the trestle blockage, or perhaps because we sought distraction from the miserable conditions (too hot to keep the windows closed, too dusty to open them), we roused ourselves from our travel-weary stupor. Monique and I talked with Hien about our past development work failures. All had occurred exactly at the moment in which we now found ourselves—the moment at which the solution (aka the "truth") is discovered. The next, almost reflexive step was to go out and spread the word: teach people, tell them, educate them. Bingo! Reflecting on those failures, we realized that they occurred because we were acting as though once people "know" something it results in their "doing" something. By the time we reached Hanoi this wide-ranging discussion was distilled into an epiphany, despite our fatigue and grittiness. What we needed to do was create an opportunity for people to practice, rather than merely know about, the successful PD behaviors the villagers had just discovered.

The objective, of course, was to rehabilitate the malnourished kids. Simple enough. That part required only the provision of sufficient additional nutritious food. The real challenge was to enable the parents to sustain their kids' enhanced nutritional status at home after rehabilitation. To address the issue of sustainability, the program would have to avoid the pitfalls the villagers had previously experienced with the supplemental feeding programs. That meant they would have to acquire new habits and change their behavior. They would have to do something different from what they were currently doing.

The newly identified PD behaviors provided the "something different." Addition of a small handful of shrimps or crabs and greens, in combination with increased frequency of feeding and other uncommon caring behaviors, had been shown to be sufficient to keep a child well nourished. We knew these foods and behaviors were accessible to even the poorest families in the village. Getting parents and caretakers of malnourished children to adopt these new foods and behaviors, however, was another matter. As noted earlier, these ingredients were not conventionally fed to children. The idea of doing so seemed as far-fetched to many as feeding garden snails (enjoyed by the French as escargots) and dandelion leaves (which garnish signature salads) to the children of Westerners. Delicacies? Maybe. But try selling that concept to your two-year-old and you have your work cut out for you!

Ever mindful of the "no impact–no visa" challenge, our first inclination (given the previous epiphany on the road to Hanoi) was to design an action learning program to enable the caregivers of malnourished children to access and practice the desired behaviors. But recent insight that success would require *doing* (the how), not just *knowing*, restrained us from laying out our optimal design. We realized that *if we designed it, it would be ours, not theirs*.

The Tedious Work of Enrollment

Imagine spending two precious weeks "enrolling people" as the visa clock was ticking away. We met with local leaders, volunteers, clinic staff, and small groups of interested villagers. Over and over, we asked: "We have all learned many valuable secrets from the villagers over the past two months about how to have a well-nourished child despite poverty. But we don't know the best way to help people to practice them. What should we do?" Although the repetition was tedious, for each new group of villagers the questions were new, and the invitation to create their own program revolutionary. (At one of the last meetings, I was barely able to repeat the same introduction yet again; to maintain my sanity, I joked in English— knowing that only the translator would get the joke—"We have come to steal your land and take your women!" Hien, without missing a beat, translated into Vietnamese, "We have learned many new valuable secrets about how to have a well-nourished child . . . ")

By the end of the second week, and scores of meetings later, a design emerged: for two weeks every month, mothers or other caretakers would bring their malnourished children to a neighbor's house for a few hours every day. Together with the health volunteer, they prepared and fed a nutritious, supplemental meal to their children. (As noted earlier, tofu or egg was provided by Save the Children to help bring children up to normal weight for their sex and age.) The moms or caretakers (very often an older sibling or a grandmother was the secondary caretaker) practiced cooking new recipes with the health volunteers and also learned and applied basic sanitation and child care practices. These sessions provided an opportunity to practice successful behaviors identified during the positive deviance inquiry, such as active feeding and washing the caretakers' and children's hands with soap and water over the course of the meal whenever they touched an unclean object.

For the caretakers, the sessions provided a legitimate "productive" activity, but one that also happened to be fun. The Vietnamese are extremely hard-working people. With their Confucian heritage overlaid with decades of communist focus on *sản xuất* (productivity), villagers rarely indulge in anything that is not productive. The little kids loved the party atmosphere of the sessions, and often "terrible eaters" astonished their moms by becoming "marathon eaters" as they competed with eight or nine other happily chewing kids.

Here was cause for celebration. We were getting caretakers to bring their kids to the monthly two-week sessions. They were being rehabilitated through the provision of additional food *plus* the PD practices. But we still faced the challenge of ensuring that they continue those practices at home after the sessions.

Price of Admission

It was the concern for the sustainability of behavioral change that led to the introduction of the mandatory "daily contribution" component of the nutrition sessions. Every day, each mother or caretaker was required to bring a handful of shrimps, crabs, or greens as the price of admission to the sessions. For two weeks every month, someone in the family (a spouse, an older sibling) had to go out to the rice paddy early in the morning and, ankle deep in mud, collect the required shrimps or crabs. By the time the two-week program was over for that month, the trip to the rice paddy with a small net and empty container had become routine.

It would be another dozen years before we found a succinct phrase that captured all this. But we had hit upon a pivotal insight: *It's easier to act your way into a new way of thinking, than to think your way into a new way of acting.* The daily contribution was a beachhead in forming new habits. Once PD behaviors have been discovered, the design must provide those who seek to learn with both the opportunity and the means to practice the new behavior. A focus on practice rather than knowledge has proven to be a key element in bringing about lasting behavioral change across the range of issues addressed using the PD methodology.

One of the other great reinforcers of behavioral change is the ability of people to see results. All children were weighed on the first and last day of the two-week nutrition session. Typically, moms and health volunteers gathered around the scale, like a crowd at a lottery scratching the numbers on their card just before the drawing. All waited for the needle to come to rest. The result? Three-quarters of kids put on weight. Each weighing was greeted with applause and cheers. Seeing that new behaviors had actually resulted in their kids gaining weight and becoming "naughtier" (active and lively rather than apathetic and listless), caretakers returned home committed to practicing their newly acquired methods. Children who reached normal nutritional status during the first nutrition session "graduated." Those who remained malnourished were signed up for the next session to be held the following month.

Community monitoring of the progress of each child's nutritional status was a critical element of the overall success and sustainability of the program. Each health volunteer carried her own growth-monitoring book with fold-out pages, enabling her to record and track the weight and nutritional status of each child in her hamlet over time. Weights were also captured at village-wide child growth-monitoring sessions every two months. This enabled health volunteers and local leaders to review the overall trend lines of all the young children every sixty days. "Score cards" captured each child's weight and were compiled into a village-wide tally.

With dramatic flourish, volunteers unlocked the green metal cabinet where precious scissors, tape, colored marking pens, and flip chart paper were stashed. They prepared their tallies of the latest "community children nutrition status" and updated their pie charts. These graphics were prominently posted in strategic places (such as near the meeting hall adjacent to the bust of Ho Chi Minh) and were one of the first things to greet villagers entering the clinic, Women's Union, or People's Committee offices. The charts enabled them to see nutritional gains in their hamlet as well as in the wider community over time. No Olympic scoring could have elicited more excitement than these postings.

By the fourth nutrition session in early June, five and a half months into the six-month pilot, the process seemed to have been incorporated into the village repertoire. Everyone had either a child, a relative, or a neighbor's kid participating in the program. Invariably, Monique, Hien, and I were warmly greeted. Things just couldn't have gone better.

Bliss of the Ignorant

It would be another two years before we discovered that under the façade of warmth and acceptance were serious doubts about our intentions. Earlier that spring of 1994, on the nineteenth anniversary of the "fall" or "liberation" of Saigon (depending on your point of view), a stringer for the Associated Press asked if she could visit our program to interview villagers for a story about memories of the "American War." We assured her that because people knew and trusted us, they would give her straight, unedited responses. And, indeed, they did. The AP journalist stayed in Thanh Hoa for two days and interviewed scores of villagers about the war. People recounted how they had feared and hated the Americans, although they never saw them face to face as the South Vietnamese had. They knew them only from twenty thousand feet as planes dropped bomb after bomb on Thanh Hoa Province, a major artery of the Ho Chi Minh trail. A war veteran, hobbling around on his one remaining leg, took the journalist to the statue of the "boy hero" standing prominently in the primary school courtyard. This fourteen-year-old boy lost his life when he threw his body over a group of nursery school children, saving their lives as a bomb exploded nearby.

The journalist asked how the villagers felt when the American NGO first came to the village to start the nutrition program (given their previous preconceptions of Americans). The women looked uncomfortable. After an exchange of glances for several long seconds, one began: "When we first started the program," she explained, "it was very difficult for us to get the caretakers to come. We had to constantly reassure the mothers and particularly the grandmothers that we were in charge of the food preparation and would oversee every step of the cooking." Confused about the extraordinary caution, the journalist asked for clarification. Had there been a mistake in translation?

"No," the volunteer continued, "your translator has it exactly right." She went on to explain. "When Ba Monique and Bac Jerry first came to the village, the villagers thought they seemed very kind, but they were, after all, Americans. The villagers were certain that they were there to poison the children! During the first weeks of the feeding program, volunteers actually had to eat some of the food at the beginning of each session before the caretakers would feed it to their children."

The finale of the fourth two-week nutrition session was in June 1991, five and a half months after we had arrived in the country. The Thanh Hoa health staff were coming to the villages to see if we had met our impact goal. Just over six hundred children had participated in the first four nutrition sessions. The authorities were coming to weigh them.

While we knew the results from the bimonthly weighings and pie charts, our anxiety rose in proportion to all that was at stake. Hien, Monique, and I waited along with a group of the volunteers in the tiny health center for the district health officers to arrive. A few minutes after the appointed hour, two Jeeps arrived, carrying seven *cán bộ y tế* (health officers) dressed in white smock coats and rubber flip-flops, pads and pens in hand. Most (597 of the 600) of the children and their caretakers had been assembled by the volunteers and were all at the ready. (You don't defeat the Americans, the Chinese, the French, and the Khmer Rouge without a strong talent for mobilization.)

We had tea, waited, had another cup of tea, looked at our watches, checked the time, and continued waiting as the weighing went on. An excruciatingly long four hours later, the district health staff approached us with smiles on their faces. Congratulations all the way around. Celebratory cups of tea. Then the highest ranking of the district health staff, Bắc sĩ (Dr.) Hanh, shared the verdict: a total of 245 kids (more than 40 percent of those who had participated in the program to date) had been completely rehabilitated, and another 20 percent had moved from severe malnutrition to moderate malnutrition. "You have earned a six-month extension of your visa," he concluded.

Within two years more than a thousand children were enrolled in nutrition sessions, and 93 percent of them "graduated."[2] As families witnessed firsthand the dramatic improvement in their children's health status, the practices became the new conventional wisdom. An external evaluation of the program in 1994 by the Harvard School of Public Health found that "younger siblings, not yet born at the time of the nutrition program implementation, [were] benefiting from the same levels of enhanced nutritional status" as their older siblings.[3] This made sense. As moms succeeded in rehabilitating their kids through the use of the new PD behaviors, they continued practicing them when their next child was born. The conventional wisdom about how to care for children had changed and was now internalized. Sustainability of the nutritional gains was assured, and there was no further need for assistance within the community.

By December 1991 it was decided that the model had proven its efficacy. It was time to demonstrate that success could be replicated elsewhere. We enlisted five junior staff members from the Vietnamese National Institute of Nutrition and had them deputized to Save the Children for a period of two years. With their help, we expanded to an additional ten villages, bringing the total to fourteen.

Although the new villages were adjacent to the original ones and the resource base almost identical, we insisted that a fresh inquiry be carried out in each new village. By now it was clear to us that the process of self-discovery was every bit as important as the actual behaviors uncovered. This focus on self-discovery, reinforced over the next decade, has proven to be a key element of the PD approach. It took the villagers in the ten new communities just over a year to realize the same dramatic results as in the original four.

Momentum was triggering a seismic shift underfoot. Unbeknownst to us, our Vietnamese hosts, from the ministerial level in Hanoi down to the leaders in the village, were becoming evangelists on behalf of what was happening. They spoke at the National Health Congress with thousands in attendance, disseminated white papers, appeared on panels. With characteristic Vietnamese attention to detail, they compared the PD outcomes to those of a resource-intensive United Nations World Food Program in a neighboring village. The PD program was determined to be more accessible, sustainable, and scalable. And the Vietnamese owned it—it was their success.

Because the program site was within a day's drive from Hanoi, dozens of visitors came to call. Soon there were numerous requests from UN agencies and district and provincial health offices outside the program area for help in implementing the program in other parts of the country. Foreign delegations began to arrive—including staff from Save the Children headquarters in Connecticut, who left resolved to disseminate the idea to other regions. But as we had been so dramatically reminded during the pilot stage, people learn best by doing. We were exposed to the grave risk of being compromised by success, and struggled for a way to achieve scale given the flood of interest in learning about the PD approach.

One rainy day a Unicef representative paid a visit. We sat together inside a sky-darkened, corrugated roof hut with a group of local moms whose kids had participated in the nutrition program. The moms were animated, shouting to be heard above the hammering of the monsoon torrent on the roof. They explained how they had rehabilitated their children and how it was possible for any poor family to have a well-nourished child. They were absolutely intent on making sure that the foreign guest got it right. After an hour or so, we thanked the women and left the hut. Our drenched visitor stood transfixed, seemingly oblivious to the elements. "That was amazing!" he said. "I've never learned so much in so little time. It was a . . . a . . . a 'living university.'" A concept was born.

The Living University was built around the fourteen program villages. They provided a social laboratory for exposure to the nutrition process at different phases of implementation. Participants could learn the conceptual framework but, more importantly, participate in fieldwork in the villages and spend twelve days directly experiencing the essential components of the program.

After graduation, Living University participants (for example, teams from the People's Committee, the health services, and the Women's Union from a given district) returned to their provinces and districts to implement the PD Nutrition Program in two new villages. They then became their own "Mini Living University" for further program expansion in adjacent areas. Over the next seven years, an estimated fifty thousand children were rehabilitated through the efforts of more than four hundred Living University graduate teams. Ultimately, the program was replicated in two hundred fifty communities encompassing a population of over 2.2 million.[4]

Reflections

PD is an approach, not a model. Malleability is an essential feature of the positive deviance process. The pervasive challenge of scaling up successful models, which more often than not fail, arises when rigid orthodoxies are transplanted on foreign soil. The PD process for nutrition, in contrast, has been successfully adopted and adapted in the last decade by ministries of health, UN organizations, and local and international NGOs in forty-one countries in Africa, Asia, Latin America, and the Middle East. PD is based on the sociocultural context of each program community. It must always be, by definition, "ours," and is genetically, "culturally appropriate." PD works like nature works. Like Darwin's finches of the Galápagos Islands, each successful adaptation must be appropriate to the local ecology.

With two decades of experience and the ongoing application of the PD process to scores of issues other than nutrition, we find ourselves constantly adding to the list of lessons learned. The first application of PD in Vietnam was very much a work in progress. We learned as we stumbled, recovered, and eventually succeeded. Many of the principles highlighted in this chapter became principles only after the fact, upon reflection of what worked and what didn't. Two important insights came from the people themselves. From an exhausted volunteer, we got the importance of hearing every voice, at every stage of the process, so that people felt included in the problem definition, inquiry, discovery, findings, and implementation. From an old woman at the end of a long day, we got the importance of *doing*, as opposed to just seeing or hearing.

Measuring Progress

With malnutrition, we had stumbled upon the easiest of all possible problems. This facilitated an "early win," as contrasted to the more murky challenges since encountered. Everyone wants a healthy, well-nourished child. Eliminating malnutrition is culturally and politically acceptable and universally compelling. It is an issue around which everyone can rally. Not so easy are the many other intractable problems on the planet.

Measuring the impact of a nutrition program is as simple as putting a child on a scale and waiting for the measuring needle to come to rest. Ability to measure is a powerful reinforcer of behavioral change. Not only is measurement simple and easily understandable to caregivers, but change is rapid. In two weeks a child can gain a few hundred grams. A caretaker witnesses not only the progress on a weight chart, but the change in the behavior of her child. One of our favorite "complaints" from participating moms, especially grandmothers, was, "Our little one is 'naughty' now." (One ruefully observed she needed a fitness program to carry the heavier child.) The listless two-year-old who had begun the program a short month or two earlier was transformed into an active, happy kid who had to be stopped from romping through the rice paddies and squashing newly planted seedlings.

Many of the subsequent issues for which the PD process has been used have been much more daunting, the constellation of potential factors impacting the problem less clear, and proof of success more diffuse. What motivates poor parents in a developing country to sell their daughter to the sex trade? Is it not Allah's will that decides the fate of infants in Pakistan? What stakeholders need to be involved to challenge the conventional wisdom? What social, economic, and cultural factors need to be explored? Determinants are a lot more complicated to spot than quantifiable factors like adding shrimps and crabs to rice in Vietnam or ladling soup from the bottom of a kettle in Bolivia. It's much more difficult to prove an event averted, as contrasted to alleviating one that occurs. Clear-cut correlations between new practices and results are more elusive. A death avoided is much more difficult to link to newly practiced behaviors than a gain in body weight.

Acting Your Way into a New Way of Thinking

"A thousand seeings aren't worth one doing." The Vietnamese proverb uttered by a humble village volunteer has become a mantra that has spawned a thousand applications around the world. It triggered our epiphany on the long drive back to Hanoi; it led to volunteer-designed workshops. It gave rise to the Living University.

Peel the onion and, not surprisingly, the concept harnesses incontrovertible principles of social psychology: *Enactment* (behaving differently in front of your peers is the shortest distance to thinking differently) and *consistency* (having staked out a position, we strive to behave accordingly).[5]

Enactment means putting skin in the game. Doing so breeds commitment—and with commitment comes a shift in attitude. The power of commitment to transform beliefs and behavior is starkly evident in experiences such as Marine boot camp, college hell week, and tribal initiation rites.[6] When people go through a lot of pain or effort to attain something, they tend to value it more highly than when it is provided with minimum effort. (Perhaps that's why expert advice and "best practices" often don't stick—no pain, no gain.) The arduous first steps of a PD process—weighing children, conducting multiple group discussions to establish common practices, and ferreting out potential PD behavior through follow-up sessions—invisibly serve to extract commitment.

The feeding workshops were based on practice—both collecting shrimps, crabs, and greens and getting one child to eat them. Practice sneaks up on you, providing a circuitous path to deep insight. For a while it's all disjointed fragments (as in the movie *Karate Kid*—"waxing on and waxing off"). Then one day, everything falls into place. Previous self-conscious activities become sublimated into your repertoire in ways that cannot be precisely explained. This is the real nature of learning.

Enactment is most effective in shifting a person's attitudes, self-image, and behavior if involvement is active, public, and effortful. A PD process fires on all three cylinders. Participants *own* their choice to be involved. The kickoff meeting and subsequent PD workshops entail small investments of individual time and attention. Slowly and gradually participants morph from observer to activist. The process also catalyzes the energies of the collective, subtly shifting group norms and assumptions from fatalism to curiosity, and the social political structures from more formal hierarchies to open systems in which the least empowered participants can offer the most important findings.

Consistency exploits another potent mechanism for attitude change. We desire to see ourselves as internally coherent and outwardly dependable. Abundant evidence shows that once we have made a choice or taken a stand, we incur both internal and interpersonal pressures to behave consistently with that commitment. Most of us look closely at our own actions and decide on that basis who we are. Consistency is a valued personality trait. Inconsistency engenders distrust.

One perverse but compelling illustration of the power of consistency derives from the experience of POWs (prisoners of war) during the Korean War. Robert Cialdini, author of *Influence: The Psychology of Persuasion*, documents the experience of captured American soldiers in POW camps run by the Chinese. "The Chinese were very effective in getting Americans to inform on one another," states Cialdini, "in striking contrast to the behavior of American POWs in World War II. For this reason, among others, escape plans were quickly uncovered and the escape attempts themselves were almost always unsuccessful. Nearly all American prisoners in the Chinese camps collaborated with the enemy in one form or another."[7]

The Chinese treated captives quite differently from their allies, the North Koreans, who employed deprivation and harsh punishment to gain compliance. Cialdini observes that by avoiding the appearance of brutality, the Chinese "lenient policy" was a sophisticated psychological assault on individual identity. The Chinese methods subtly harnessed the human quest for psychological consistency. They'd ask prisoners to make statements that seemed inconsequential ("the U.S. is not perfect; Communism may be a good form of government for some societies"). If a soldier agreed, he might be asked to give examples. The next step was to get the POW to write these concessions down or verbalize these admissions with other POWs in a group. (Those who refused were asked to copy the statements of others.) Then, to the POW's surprise, written statements might be read to the whole camp on the PA system or used on an anti-American radio show (overheard by U.S. intelligence agencies along with the POW's name, rank, and serial number).[8]

Henry Segal and Edgar Schein, who headed the psychological evaluation team that examined returning POWs at the war's end, noted how self-image is squeezed from both sides by consistency pressures. From the inside, there is a pressure to bring self-image into line with action. From the outside, there is a social pressure—a tendency to adjust this image according to the way others perceive us. And because others see us as believing what we have written or said (even when we've had little choice in the matter), we experience a pull to bring self-image into line with the written statement.[9]

The pilot PD process in Vietnam surely drew on the consistency principle—although not with manipulative intentions. Villagers took public stands in volunteering for the initiative, demonstrating further investment through weighing kids and facilitating group discussions on common practices and prospective PDs. Unsurprisingly, when the need arose for sponsors and activists for the feeding workshops, consistency pressures guided their ongoing involvement as surely as a gyroscope on a Mars-bound spacecraft holds to its trajectory. Unlike in Korea, where consistency was manipulated to an adversary's advantage, in the PD process we seek to avoid manipulation by insisting that the community, and *only* the community, decides whether and what it will pursue.

As noted in chapter 1, PD makes sense when a problem is "adaptive" as contrasted to "technical." What distinguishes one from the other is *social complexity* and the need for *behavioral change*. In Vietnam, had the solution been the introduction of high-yield or drought-resistant rice, social and behavioral change by the villagers would have been unnecessary. But we learned to be alert to the way in which "logical" technical solutions can inflict a kind of cognitive blindness. The elegance and efficiency of technical solutions seduces us—preventing the change advocate from spotting the behavioral and social land mines along the way. The Salk vaccine eliminated polio. Seems straightforward. But recent outbreaks in India and Nigeria underscore that superstitions regarding vaccine use by some rural communities have allowed a disease largely eliminated from the planet to stage a comeback. Problems embedded in social and behavioral patterns resist technical fixes. Valid technical solutions pass without impact through a resistant social system like neutrons through a concrete building.

The "Expert" Trap

The villagers' prior experience with nutritional and agricultural experts had not been good. We noted how expert status, in and of itself, can shift the ownership from the community to dependence on the expert's authority. We witnessed what was possible when villagers engaged in the learning process and discovered the solutions for themselves. The outsider's "expertise" spares the community from the essential trial and error of learning.

The larger point here: too often those in sponsorship, expert, or author-ity roles can generate unconstructive dependency among their followers. This dependency can absolve the community from owning the solutions it must adopt for change to succeed. When the group becomes the guru, members "credientialize" themselves as change agents. We learned in Viet-nam that problem identification, ownership, and action must begin in and remain with the community. Community members are the opportunity and the source. When the villagers stepped up and became accountable for the design of the feeding workshops, they introduced nuances that would have been hard to grasp from afar—let alone implement top-down. Disbelief and resistance dissipated like morning mist over the rice fields.

The Problem of Scaling

A "product warning" is in order here. PD successes scale far better "vertically" (i.e., within the community involved) than they do horizontally (i.e., replicating successes across communities). The reason is self evident: each community must opt in to the process and discover its unique wisdom for the discoveries to gain traction.[10] The future is created one community at a time. Each defines its own future, and pilots its own destiny.

The conundrum arises when trying to apply "shrimps, crabs, and greens" from one Vietnamese village to the next. Without careful attention to the setup (beginning with a group decision to opt in to the process and invest sweat equity in determining *their own* common practices and dis-covering uncommon ones), the unfolding pattern quickly defaults to a "best practices" drill. Ownership is absent or insufficient to sustain inter-est, immune responses are activated, and fleeting curiosity ebbs away.

Each community's stakeholders, group dynamics, and solutions are exquisitely idiosyncratic. The good news: once people have tasted self-generated success and flourished from their own wisdom, the foundation for learning is laid. Throughout the world, villages and organizations that have been the beneficiaries of PD continue to evolve as they apply the process to other intractable problems.

Finale

In June 1996 Monique and I left Hanoi for Cairo. Hanoi had not been a comfortable place to live. Our tiny, eight-hundred-square-foot concrete apartment, unheated in winter and stifling in summer, would not be missed. Nor would the constant government surveillance of our activities, the parade of visitors to our home, telephone calls at all hours of the night, and incoming and outgoing telegrams. And yet, the thought of leaving our friends, our work, and the villagers with whom we had shared so much during our weekly visits, of relinquishing our current life, was wrenching.

We had come to cherish Hien as our younger sister and guardian angel. We would sorely miss our hot-chili-for-breakfast-lunch-and-dinner driver Dinh; our former library-archivist-turned-housekeeper Huong; our officemates and friends; Lang, the English Department chairwoman at the Hanoi College (now working with us as trainer and head of the Living University); and Tuan, a nuclear physicist (who joined us as a secretary to earn a decent living but was swiftly promoted to senior staff member).

We somehow made it through the final few weeks of formal and informal parties and farewells. On our very last evening in Hanoi, we had a gathering of our closest Vietnamese and expatriate friends. Those goodbyes were the hardest, and we couldn't bear the thought of having to go through them yet again. We pleaded with our friends not to come to the airport the next morning. Our expatriate friends understood and complied. But it was just too much to ask of our Vietnamese friends, for whom an uncelebrated departure would have been a grievous, unthinkable act of disrespect.

As we arrived at the airport the next morning, two vans full of our Vietnamese friends showed up bearing enormous bouquets of roses, flower leis, and kilos of our favorite dried shiitake mushrooms to say their final "final goodbyes." Long hugs, and tears. Then, without turning back, we made our way through passport control and customs, and onto Thai Airways for the first leg of our journey to our next destination, Cairo.

Waiting on the runway, sealed within our "smooth as silk" cabin, we already seemed worlds removed from the bustling contradictions of Hanoi on the other side of the window: its entrepreneurship checked by Marxist orthodoxy, passion and sensuality stirring within prudish restraint, an irrepressible spirit infecting the somber rectitude, transitioning forward yet holding back. Monique and I sat in silence while the pilot intoned, "Cabin crew, be seated for takeoff." Six years of our lives had been spent in Vietnam. We had learned more there than anywhere else in our professional lives. Vietnam had given us the opportunity to embark on the PD journey, which has shaped our lives ever since. Takeoff; wheels up, in the air, and off into the unknown.

THREE

Female Circumcision in Egypt

Reconciling Tradition and Change

Cultures have their layers of complexity, but some are more labyrinthine than others. The first weeks in Cairo were packed with official meetings and social gatherings, introducing a network of contacts from across the city's social strata. The welcome featured the grace and hospitality for which Egyptians are renowned. But it would not be long before complex undercurrents would bubble up through surface impressions. Beneath the layer of authentic courtesy lay deeper challenges and conventions of Egyptian life. As Monique describes, all this proved relevant in applying the positive deviance process to a seemingly intractable problem in Egypt.

FEMALE GENITAL MUTILATION (FGM) is the surgical removal of part or all of the external female genitalia. The practice traces to pharaonic times, and has existed for thousand of years. Every year, 3 million girls in twenty-eight countries in Africa are subjected to the practice, as are thousands of girls in immigrant communities in Europe, North America, and Australia. Globally between 100 and 140 million girls and women have been cut or mutilated.[1]

In Egypt, as of 1997, ninety-seven percent of ever-married or marriage-eligible women between the ages of fifteen and forty-nine had undergone some form of the procedure.[2] Performed during adolescence, circumcision is most commonly referred to as *Il Rittan* (excision). It is woven into the fabric of Egyptian life and culture. The practice transcends social, economic, and educational boundaries. Daughters of lawyers and peasants, illiterate and highly educated women, village dwellers and Cairennes are subjected to the practice. Accepted by Christians and Muslims alike, female circumcision has been highly resistant to change. FGM is so widely accepted that three-quarters of Egyptian women view it as a means of enhancing health and hygiene (i.e., to keep the genital area clean and "prevent the clitoris from growing like a penis").

For Khira, it all started the day after Easter, an important time of joy and celebration in this traditional Coptic Christian community. As a twelve-year-old girl, she was looking forward to playing with her girlfriends. Unbeknownst to her, the holy day was also an occasion to circumcise young girls. Khira was laughing and playing with her friends when her mother, accompanied by a favorite aunt, interrupted their play, guiding them to a nearby tent. She had no idea what was about to unfold. As she approached, she noticed a small group of men, including her uncle, hovering nearby. They too were part of the plot—to catch uncooperative girls who tried to escape.

Once inside, squinting in semidarkness, Khira could make out the familiar faces of her mother, older sisters, aunts, and grandmother. Off to the side sat an unknown man next to the cot, fidgeting at a small worktable with a large basin, kettle of water, cloth, and razor. These were the tools of circumcision.

The women began whispering among themselves. Khira overheard her mother ask that her daughter go first, not knowing the request was made to ensure the straight razor be sharp, the cut swift and clean. Then, before she knew what was happening, the women had surrounded her, grabbed her arms, pulled her to the cot, and spread her legs. Terrified,

Khira fought back, kicking and screaming, her voice muffled by a firm hand and her body restrained by strong arms. The barber moved in with the knife. The pain was overpowering and she lost consciousness. She came to in a different tent, opening her eyes to her mother and grandmother's soothing voices, applying ash and onion compresses between her legs.

Khira could not walk for days. She lay in bed with her legs open so that the wound could begin to heal. Her first steps were excruciatingly painful and precarious. For months, she could not look her mother, grandmother, or her father in the eye. There were nightmares. Psychologically, she became withdrawn, less trusting, fearful that however well life might seem to be going at a particular time, something terrible lurked just around the corner. She would never fully trust her family again.

I spent my first two months in Cairo looking for a job, approaching various organizations to ask about their work on current development issues, and generally orienting myself. Key concerns were high illiteracy rates among women and poor maternal health care. Then someone mentioned FGM, the millennia-old practice of female circumcision. I followed up with members of the Egyptian task force for FGM eradication and was sobered by the legacy of meager progress, notwithstanding the decade-long efforts to curtail it.

As I listened, I flashed back to my first encounter with FGM in Mauritania. Type III circumcision (infibulation, the most severe form) is a common practice in that country, and health providers have long dealt with its traumatic and sometimes deadly side effects. We were there on behalf of the Peace Corps. I witnessed many intense debates among our young female Peace Corps health volunteers who were viscerally opposed to the practice. But custom and tradition prevailed. We were required to back off in order to ensure the volunteers remained welcome in the villages and to avoid compromising the entire Peace Corps mission.

I was astonished to learn that almost all Egyptian women were circumcised. But I could not have conceived how profoundly the scars of this
practice disfigured lives. Nor could I have imagined that the circumcised
survivors would muster the courage and perseverance to light the way for
profound social and cultural change. Looking back, it was perhaps my lack
of knowledge and reluctance to tackle this issue that allowed me to be
quiet. Listening with an open mind, I was able to gain access to the hidden
world of FGM and, ultimately, together with Egyptian colleagues, discover
the solutions from within.

As I sat in the meetings in Cairo, I began to wonder: was there a way
to use positive deviance for this very sensitive topic? Experience with the
approach in nutrition lured like a beacon in the fog, illuminating a possible
path forward. But, I thought to myself, the "positive" aspect of "deviant"
behavior is all in the eyes of the beholder. Societal acceptance of FGM in
Egypt made it more complicated than the problem of childhood malnutrition in Vietnam. In the latter instance, everyone (community, family, village, and local government) wanted to fix the problem. Who doesn't want
a well-nourished child? In contrast, FGM in Egypt is not only deeply
rooted but regarded as a desirable practice. It would be difficult, maybe
impossible, to mobilize a community around what was universally perceived as a benefit. As an outsider, who was I to question a practice that
everyone outside of the small anti-FGM community saw as a virtue? Still, I
could not ignore the statistics and the stories. They weighed on my heart
and troubled my dreams.

I attended more meetings on the subject and consistently heard anti-
FGM advocates decry imperceptible successes and failed strategies. One
day I was reviewing a report on a reproductive health education program
for adolescent girls that addressed the topic of FGM. A girl was quoted as
saying: "We know now that Il Rittan is a terrible practice. But we cannot
tell our mothers not to do it to our younger sisters. They will not listen to
us. They will say: 'Show me an uncircumcised girl who is married! Show
me a decent uncircumcised woman! Then I will believe you!'"

I caught my breath. Further down in the text another girl added her voice: "Show us the people who have not done this, show us the people who have resisted, then with proof we can tell our mothers." Goose bumps rose on my arms; my heart raced. Right there, in their own words, girls begged to identify exceptions in their own communities to help convince their mothers to stop the practice. Perhaps this was the key to the puzzle. We could help if we could find the positive deviants—those defying the norm. "Yes," a more circumspect voice in my head added, "but even if we can find them, don't underestimate the challenges of overturning a four-thousand-year-old tradition."

Controlling girls' virginity and women's sexuality are the main justifications for the practice. Most women believe that they are circumcised out of the need to fulfill social obligations of purity, honor, and marriage-ability, because traditionally men refuse to marry uncircumcised girls. Additionally, neighbors look upon the family of the uncircumcised with suspicion. Needless to say, bucking this hard-held practice is perceived as ill advised, self-destructive—indeed, almost unimaginable. So the cycle continues. Fear of being socially ostracized motivates families and individuals to perpetuate it. Excision is seen as a critical safeguard based on the belief that uncircumcised women have abnormal sexual appetites that will make them prone to commit adultery. Finally, there is the counterintuitive conviction that "cutting is caring." Mothers often say they circumcise their daughters "out of love."

Surprisingly, "modernized" lives and increased social mobility for women have not been an FGM deterrent but rather made it easier to perform. Nowadays, the trend is to have the girl circumcised by a doctor or health provider, the circumcision rendered less *physically* painful by use of local anesthesia. Moreover, the trend of more daughters leaving the village to work in cities and be educated compels families to circumcise them because it is perceived as a guarantee necessary to preserve the girl's virginity.

At best, the harsh reality of genital cutting leaves women with decreased sexual sensation and suppressed sexual drive, often compounded, as described earlier, by traumatic psychological and emotional scarring that does not disappear. At worst, there is serious infection, hemorrhage, and sometimes death. The psychological scarring carries over to the relationships they will forge with their future husbands. As one young woman confided in her soft, tentative voice: "It is a wound that never heals."

In rural areas, circumcision traditionally takes place at the end of the month, or sometimes on the occasion of a local saint's celebration festival. As in Khira's story, women get together and decide whose daughters will be circumcised together. This is seen as creating a bond among them (an event referred to as *mushahree*). The girls are usually between nine and thirteen years old and belong to the same clan. Then the women choose a person to perform the operation, usually the *daya* (traditional birth attendant) or the barber. Unlike many rites of passage, the act is conceived in secrecy from its victims. This clandestine prelude to the trauma causes girls to experience shock, then shame. Hemorrhage and infection are not uncommon. They refer to the time of circumcision as "the dark day."

Small Steps, Long Journey

Alone in my office, reading through field interviews, a persistent pattern emerged from the telling. Woman after woman recounted a world upended, fear and searing pain, then subsequent feelings of shame and betrayal that did not lessen with time. The life stories began to merge and mingle. Past and present, young and old. My silent office was filled with their voices, some pleading for confirmation that the practice was wrong. This repressed cry for help sought a breach in the wall of societal imperatives, an opening for the girls' pleas to be not just heard but acknowledged and acted on. Emboldened by their anguish, I resolved to try to tackle the issue with a PD approach.

While my desire to do something kept me awake at night, it was accompanied by a great deal of self-questioning. What were the unintended consequences of taking action? What if the identities of the individuals and families were revealed to their communities? If informants were found out, what repercussions might follow? Tackling the topic was dangerous and involved great risk.

I was introduced to the leader of the Egyptian task force against FGM, and explained a bit about PD and how it might be used to address the issue of FGM. I was then invited to address the membership at large. Turning the problem on its head, I presented the assembled with the upending PD question: "Rather than focusing on the 97 percent of women who are circumcised," I suggested, "can we look and learn from the 3 percent who are not—the three to five hundred thousand uncircumcised Egyptian women and their families who, as we speak, have managed to resist the practice?"

After a long pause, they responded with an enthusiastic "yes!" But in Egypt, as in many nations of the world, verbal endorsement often substitutes for the resources and commitment necessary to actually do something. The task force suggested I research and document the existence of positive deviants and the factors that enabled them to avoid circumcision. I countered that the positive deviance approach doesn't use an outside expert to build the case; it engages local organizations, and through them, members of the community. Their response was immediate and emphatic: this option would not work. Ending further discussion on the matter, the informal leader flatly concluded: "No insider will touch it; it is too dangerous!"

I began to make inquiries among women's advocacy organizations to find out if any would work with me in such an enterprise. It was tough going. Resistance was so strong and rejection so universal that I began to question the undertaking. I thought about giving up. Then one day I was having lunch with the head of the local Center for Development and Population Activities office (CEDPA). CEDPA staff had taken on the issue of FGM in Egypt through their adolescent girl's reproductive health education program. Knowing that they were well aware of the obstacles, I felt free to vent my frustration. The director interrupted my rant midsentence: "Let's try it!" Abruptly, a roadblock had dissolved. The first major obstacle—finding a local sponsor—had been surmounted.

With a small grant dedicated specifically to FGM eradication, CEDPA laid the groundwork for a pilot with a yet-to-be-determined partner. Now we needed to assemble a core team. The pool of "applicants" was not very large. (Most candidates were terrified to touch the subject.) We ended up with four very diverse individuals: Romany, Shahira, Soumaia, and myself. Initially, the only common denominator was our title: "the PD team." None of us had any previous direct experience working with FGM.

Romany was a jovial and sensitive man who supervised the program activities implemented by CEDPA's partner organizations. His wide smile and soothing voice were invaluable attributes in dissipating tension and building trust. A Coptic by religion, Romany quickly embraced the PD concept, took on a team leadership role, and always found a positive way to approach challenges.

Soumaia was still recovering from a serious car accident that left her in constant pain. She was very religious, and Christianity fueled her resolve in life. Though she was not an instinctive PD champion, she had signed on to make it work. As the most guarded team member, she refused to share her experiences with "it." As a skeptic, she challenged our assumptions, questioned our strategies, and kept us on our toes.

Shahira came to the team as my interpreter. A devout Muslim and a medical doctor, Shahira wore the veil. Her shroud transfixed the onlooker's attention on her big, intelligent blue eyes. She spoke fluent French (my native language), having attended a French Catholic school as is the custom among the Cairo elite. This bond proved an important one, transforming a collegial relationship into a lasting friendship. Remarkably, at thirty-five, Shahira claimed to know little of female circumcision (perhaps testimony to her embarrassment to admit its prevalence to a Westerner). If you're not on the inside, you don't hear a lot about it. She overcame whatever obstacles stood in her way and immersed herself in statistics and stories that couldn't lie. She became a passionate advocate against the practice. As a very skilled translator, she played a pivotal liaison role between me (the foreigner), our Egyptian partners, and the broader community.

Then there I was, declared religious agnostic, foreigner, a woman, and a Westerner to boot. Here was the "expert" in an approach with an oxymoronic name, intent on applying it to a practice where no one had gone before. To minimize outsider influence on the process, I became technical advisor to the team. As a non-Egyptian, I had severe cultural and linguistic limitations. Humbled by the audacity of the experiment and daunted by its cultural sensitivity, I usually refrained from rendering judgments, offering opinions, or making suggestions. This was an Egyptian problem that only Egyptians could solve.

The PD team's first meeting was consummated by a very Egyptian custom: sharing a take-out meal in the office. We would dine together at every opportunity. It helped build relationships, consolidate our team, define roles, and developed trust. Trust became the sine qua non in the endeavor. I had to trust my team, and they me and the process. They would be my eyes, translate my voice, and adopt my expertise as one guides a blind person through a maze.

Search for a Beta Site

With conviction outweighing the uphill journey before us, we also began casting about for a local NGO that would be willing to pilot PD at the community level. This was a crucial step: finding a local partner willing to collaborate on a "taboo issue" and willing to suspend disbelief (given that we had no proven blueprint in this arena or evidence of prior success).

The prevailing code of silence around FGM made the search extremely difficult. Many doors closed after a polite first meeting. The (predominantly male) leaders of many of these local organizations reacted with amazement at the audacity of the endeavor. Amazement soured into incredulity when told that not only were some Egyptian women not circumcised, but overwhelmingly, most women in the world were not either. One director fixed me directly with his eyes as if to administer a lie detector test: "Aren't you circumcised?" he asked. "No. In France, no women are circumcised," I responded. He was dumbstruck and, after an awkward silence, excused himself. Remaining behind, his female assistant, present throughout and listening intently, timidly asked: "If you are not circumcised, don't you want sex all the time?" "No, sometimes I have a headache," I retorted. This was received with much laughter, proof that some feminine strategies are universal.

The Coptic Organization for Services and Training (COST) is a Christian organization run by a very charismatic nun named Sister Yoanna. COST had been actively involved in advocacy activities against FGM for years, partnering with many local communities. It had hosted awareness meetings and expert lectures from doctors and religious leaders. Attendees typically listened politely and expressed commitment to change—then circumcised their daughters. Simply transmitting "knowledge" was not working.

Sister Yoanna expressed an immediate willingness to consider this risky venture when everyone else we approached would not. Her order was devoted to the alleviation of suffering. FGM curtailment had been a decade-long priority toward this end, but all prior efforts had met with little success. In a culture of authority-driven change, the idea that there were people in the community who had resisted the practice intrigued her. We explored ways to introduce the PD approach to potential volunteers in a way that would be culturally accessible and compelling. After much deliberation, we conclude that, if we could identify them, actual testimony of PDs themselves was our best hope.

But, did they exist? Would they be willing to divulge their uncircumcised status or anti-FGM convictions? Given the anticipated magnitude of cultural disbelief, we would need to have compelling evidence. (Even if we could find women willing to talk, no one would take our word for it.) Romany proposed videotaping PD interviews. We tried this idea on the FGM task force. They rejected it out of hand: "You must be joking! You will not find anybody willing to talk on video!" Discounting orthodoxies, I challenged team members to determine whether this counsel was valid. In unison, they balked, declaring it not just socially awkward but a surefire showstopper. Reluctantly, perhaps not wanting to disappoint me and expecting their findings to bring me to my senses, one by one they acquiesced and agreed to search for potential candidates. We committed to reconvene after two weeks and give it a try.

When we met again, both men and women had been identified—an astonishingly diverse group of individuals from urban and rural areas—who were willing to talk. The sample included a grandmother, parents who refused to circumcise their daughters, a man married to an uncircumcised woman, and a medical doctor who had stopped practicing FGM. Two of the prospects had university degrees, two were chairmen of local community development agencies, two were semiliterate. Most important, all agreed to be videotaped. From these volunteers we selected six on the basis of the complementarity of their narratives and logistical practicality. Against all odds, we seemed ready to launch our program.

As we were about to videotape our first interview, an unforeseen problem arose: the first woman would not speak in front of a stranger operating the camera. Serendipitously, one of our team knew her and could fill in as camera operator.

We learned a lot from this first session. It was extremely awkward for men and women to speak openly about their "deviant" status, especially live on camera. Thereafter, to build rapport and foster trust before the taping, we held preliminary meetings to create a safe environment, lower stress, and put respondents at ease. Subsequent videotapings went off without a hitch. Soon we had a repository of testimony and a staff emboldened by a new sense of purpose. It was time for the next step.

Make It Safe to Learn

Many big problems go unresolved because the path to solution is littered with foreboding risks (emphatically the case in Egypt). When new ways of doing things are contemplated, the prospect of change can evoke conflicting loyalties and catapult people from their comfort zone. These are but a few of the reasons why change is difficult.

Sister Yoanna, the team, and I were all aware that we were engaged in a danger sport—not only for us but for potential volunteers. Prospective positive deviants might be exposed, ridiculed, or subjected to retaliation if their advocacy challenged the status quo. Even anti-FGM advocates not involved in our project might be threatened. Yes, these authority figures might want change. But most are more comfortable when *they* impose the solutions. Some might be very uncomfortable with our bottom-up process, where they could not predict what would happen. Sister Yoanna seemed reconciled to these risks. She was willing to go with the flow rather than have all the answers.

Anxieties are often heightened when people undertake change alone. Alternatively, when members of a broader social system are engaged together, scary and disruptive aspects of change can seem less daunting. Involving a larger community in difficult work generates ownership and, more importantly, a sense of "control." Strength in numbers emboldens members to question orthodoxies and unfreezes the status quo. Momentum builds as participants feel they are driving the inquiry, not riding as passengers on somebody else's bus.

A great deal can be done to reduce these barriers by giving careful thought to the choreography of the process. Mobilizing a group requires exquisite sensitivity to the social architecture that brings people together. Considerable attention was given to the setup. We thought long and hard about whom we should involve. Inclusion must look beyond the usual suspects. Where would we meet? How would the conversation begin?

(See the box "The Choreography of a Conversation" for more details on the workshop.)

Crucial to the process is the authenticity of the invitation itself. Once the curious and potentially committed have been introduced to the concept of PD and examples from other settings, those assembled are *truly*

The Choreography of a Conversation

The last day of the workshop set aside a significant amount of practice time for participants to train in listening techniques, as none had any previous experience. The methodology draws heavily on the large body of experience with community building—Marvin Weisberg, Saul Alinsky, Dan Yankelovich, and Peter Block, to name a few of the major contributors.

We began by discussing the way we connect with people. We explored trust building by asking participants to relate their own experiences with building trust. The participants shared stories (e.g., striking up a conversation with a stranger on a bus). Patterns of engagement emerged: the importance of space, pacing the conversation, not rushing headlong into direct questions, asking open-ending questions, lingering on small talk, finding an opening where the conversation flows naturally.

The group now moved to videotaping role plays based on anticipated scenarios. Story lines eased the participants' visible anxiety at broaching the topic of circumcision. It enabled them to practice the behaviors they had just been discussing, not least of which was the palliative effect of humor. Laughter is the shortest distance between two people. It lowers tension and puts people at ease. After each practice session, feedback was exchanged, improving the quality of the interviews.

empowered to opt in or opt out. (That's the authentic meaning of an "invitation"—you get to accept or decline. "No" must be a viable, politically acceptable option for commitment to be real.)

The Monastery

With Sister Yoanna in the lead, we choreographed a PD workshop with COST staff and community development partners from two villages. It would be held in a most unlikely place: a Coptic monastery on the banks of the Nile near the town of Beni Suef. For security reasons, Sister Yoanna sought the seclusion and the symbolic safety of its thick protective walls for the three-day event. Had the authorities learned of our plans, the whole project would have been shut down. In Egypt, under law, NGOs must inform the local authorities of any activity or training they undertake.

During the three-and-a-half-hour car trip between Cairo and Beni Suef, our team was unusually silent—nervous about what we were about to do. We felt unprepared and apprehensive about what might happen. "What ifs" had kept me awake until dawn. A skeptical voice kept telling me this was none of my business. Despite hours of planning, maybe we couldn't measure up to the task.

On a blustery December day, the cold mitigated by a spirited bird's song piercing the monastery silence, we gathered as coconspirators. Shivering was as much from fear and anxiety as from the freezing temperatures. I contemplated the small desert lark in the monastery's inner courtyard, its resonant call belying its small size. Our voices, too, sought to shatter the silence of a centuries-old taboo. Like the lark, we felt small and fragile before the daunting ramparts of custom.

Thanks to the advance work of our community partners, eighteen volunteers gathered in the monastery that day, including representatives from the village community, our team, COST staff, and Sister Yoanna herself. Community members came from the villages of Ezbet Girgis and Abu

Hashem. As a bystander, I observed in the initial hours how individuals gravitated to each other for comfort and release from their anxiety. Staff huddled separately on one side of the room and villagers on the other. We were challenging well-established norms by bringing together local NGO staff and villagers. This, alone, was a totally new experience for them. Breaking from tradition so ingrained and pervasive would require creating a whole new way of connecting and speaking to each other. We would need to bridge class boundaries and the gender divide. We needed to create trust among participants who were to engage in disclosure that was, in itself, a tacit betrayal of community norms. Two of the youngest participants—Khira, from Abu Hashem village, and Warda, from Ezbet Girgis—sat apart from the adults, talking furtively to each other, eyes averted. They looked uneasy and pale. Was I imagining sadness? What was their story? Why were they here?

We began sharing personal stories to establish common experiences across separate lives. We dug into purses and wallets for pictures, each person producing family photos, which were shared about the room. Stilted formal conversation turned to anecdotes about loved ones, lives, dreams for our children, nieces, and nephews. The room became warmer. We described previous situations that made the PD process real. Should the group participants decide to take the initiative forward and discover the solutions, they would decide what happens next.

A mind-clearing feature of the PD process is the focus on the problem itself. Samuel Johnson once observed that "nothing focuses the mind like a hanging in the morning." Morbid imagery aside, the quote captures the essence of the matter. If these volunteers could acknowledge the consequences of FGM as real, important enough to tackle, and invest the effort to do so, I knew that many of today's seemingly insurmountable obstacles would fade into the background. Social systems reconfigure themselves in mysterious ways and its members are borne along in its wake.

With the group more relaxed, we began playing the videotapes. Participants watched and listened intently, looking slightly stunned and uneasy as personal details were disclosed. When the video ended, we asked for reactions. To our amazement, their first impulse was textbook shock, anger, and rejection. "Why did you show us these people? *They are actors!* Why are they talking about Il Rittan that way?" It took a lot to convince the assembled that these were ordinary people talking about their personal experiences with sincere emotions and feelings. Interesting! Speaking out against Il Rittan was inconceivable, even for those disposed to question it.

Our responses managed to erect a tentative bridge over the credibility gap. The group now asked to see the tape again. We obliged. This time the enormity of what they had witnessed began to span the abyss of disbelief. Questions flew. "How has this been possible?" "How did you find such people?" "What made these people tell their stories to you?"

We explained how we had found volunteers and the circumstances under which they had agreed to be videotaped. Sister Yoanna drove to the core of the matter: "How did these people come to trust you?" I answered the question with a question: "Exactly, how do we create trust? What does it take to create an atmosphere where people will talk?" Everyone had a view about this. Subgroup conversations began simultaneously. The room soon filled with the din of that uniquely Egyptian pattern of holding intimate conversations in the midst of cacophony.

Dinner came. Emotionally charged but exhausted, we inhaled a hearty meal prepared by the nuns consisting of lentil soup, boiled mutton, pasta, and rice. Heartfelt laughter, celebration, and release filled the monastery dining hall. We felt ourselves on the brink of something big. After dinner, the group went outside and lingered in silence, watching the last embers of the setting sun sparkling on the swollen Nile.

Back in the chamber, two kerosene lamps provided feeble illumination. A woman whispered to our translator that she had a story to share. She began: "What I am going to tell you, I have never shared with anyone, not with any member of my family, not even with my dearest sister." Lowering her eyes, her gaze fixed on trembling hands gathered self-consciously in her lap, words tumbled out one after the other. She described the day she was circumcised at the age of twelve.

"I can't forget that day. It is the darkest day in my life. I felt humiliated and ashamed. It was Eid time [a Muslim holiday]. My aunt came by and said: 'Come and bake cookies at my house.' So I went there and found other girls from the same age all from our family clan. They put us in one room with the *daya* and some women relatives. Before my turn, I had to watch the circumcision being done on one of my relatives. I screamed and knocked on the door trying to escape the scene, but with no success. I bled for almost ten days before they took me to the hospital. Afterwards, I was afraid to even go past my aunt's house."

When she finished, eyes were filled with tears and most cheeks moist. A prolonged reflective silence filled the room. Then the dam was broken. Another participant began to talk about her ambivalence about the practice. Another spoke, and then another. The groundswell of openness and sharing extended well into the night. Khira and Warda kept to themselves and remained quiet and uncomfortable.

The next morning, the atmosphere among the group was markedly different. The tension and anxiety of the first day had dissipated. Breaking the code of silence about Il Rittan and sharing personal experiences had created a common bond.

Day two commenced with a discussion of the origins of FGM and its current practice in Egypt. Participants were asked to break into small groups and profile its ramifications in their communities. Later they shared the highlights with everyone. Some spoke about their experience in advocating against the practice, highlighting the difficulties and obstacles they had encountered along the way.

Later in the afternoon, attention turned back to the individual testimony they had seen on the video screen. We asked: "What is a suitable name for these people?" The group converged on the Arabic term for "role model." (The term *positive deviant* is not acceptable in all cultures. One goes with what works.) We asked them to think about what kind of people in their communities may have refused to practice Il Rittan or stopped circumcising subsequent daughters after the first. Discussion generated a list of potential role models. The group decided collectively that, in addition to uncircumcised women and girls, individuals who had successfully convinced family members or friends not to circumcise their daughters should be included in the pool. It was further expanded to include sheikhs and priests who were known to oppose the practice.

"What about men married to uncircumcised women?" asked a male CDA staff member, talking for the first time. Also, some doctors and *dayas* are no longer willing to perform the procedure. Another girl added: "Some circumcised daughters plead successfully with their parents to spare their younger sisters." All agreed that these too were PDs in their own right. More names to the list. Questions that had never been asked evoked answers that had never been contemplated.

The group now explored how they would approach the people on their list. Their main objective, all agreed, was to ask people to tell their stories. Was there a defining moment that shaped their convictions about FGM? Once the conversation started, follow-up questions might capture successful strategies to convince others, flag the obstacles faced and how they overcame them. Finally, it was important to inquire what should be done and the role they would be willing to play. Importantly, these conversations needed to conclude with one crucial question: "Do you know others who would be willing to talk about this?"

Throughout all this, Khira and Warda remained largely silent. I sought out Shahira's insight. Only then did I learn that Khira had confided the night before that she was supposed to get married to her first cousin but had postponed the impending marriage numerous times. She was afraid of intimacy because of the trauma she had experienced during her circumcision.

Late in the evening of that productive day, other participants shared painful personal experiences. This time Khira and Warda were willing to take the floor. Surprising us all, Warda confided that she was not circumcised, until now always believing there was something wrong with her for being "uncut." Her older sister had such a terrible experience with Il Rittan she convinced their mother not to inflict this on her younger sisters. For Warda, not being circumcised meant feeling set apart from other girls, being stigmatized and fearing that she could never marry. The conversation had made her aware that her mother's abstention was an act of courage. Now she herself acknowledged a mission to go back to her community and seek out uncircumcised girls like herself.

Khira, emboldened by her friend's telling and the cocoon of trust that embraced us, recounted the painful experience that began this chapter. She ended with: "Based on what I have learned here, I have no shame now. What is shameful is what happened to me before."

By the conclusion of the workshop, participants were committed to action and sought to get started as soon as possible. They decided to meet again in six weeks to share what they had learned. Informed by experience, they would plan their next steps.

It was time to reflect on our journey. On day one, few had believed there were positive deviants in their communities. (And if so, they wouldn't talk.) By day three, every individual had identified a few PDs with whom they had personal contact. Participants shared revelations: "Why didn't I notice the positive deviants before?" "Have I been wrong all along to accept a tradition without questioning it?" Soul searching brought uneasiness and pain. For some, there was a realization: "Why are we continuing to hurt those whom we love so much?"

Equipped with skills and supported by one another, the inquiry teams set out in pairs with a daunting task ahead: identify and interview individuals in their communities who had said no to FGM. To describe them as confident and comfortable with the task would be a stretch. Many later confessed how unsure they were, frightened by the mission, and how dangerous it felt to broach a taboo subject.

We too were afraid. The enormity of our exposure didn't fully hit me until I returned to Cairo. I spent the ensuing six weeks waiting and imagining the worst. The monastery experience had demonstrated the PD process worked with the volunteers. But it had also revealed the complexity of the issue and the formidable obstacles in our path. What kept me awake was the thought that I had endangered the volunteers' personal lives. I kept telling myself to trust the people and the process. Everything would turn out all right. But sleep came fitfully.

Six interminable weeks! It was finally time to return to the monastery and hear the news. The first group to arrive was the team from Ezbet. I was stunned when they entered with additional people in tow. These prospective PDs, discovered in the interview process, now wanted to be part of our project.

Our sparse, whitewashed room was soon filled with people talking and laughing, a reunion of old friends plus a welcome to newcomers. Everyone seemed excited and impatient to talk. In sharp contrast to the stilted beginnings of the first workshop, palpable enthusiasm, hope, and a powerful sense of purpose prevailed. As we settled down, anecdotes came nonstop. Interviewers were amazed at the eagerness of individual community members to talk once they overcame the hurdle of initiating the conversation. Listeners went home and discussed what they had heard with their families. One mother asked her daughter's forgiveness for the wrong she had done. A grandmother promised to stop pressuring her daughter-in-law to have her granddaughters circumcised.

"I was always so cold with my husband, he thought I loved someone else," Om Mayada said. She understood that circumcision had severely compromised intimacy. Their sexual relationship was both emotionally troubling and psychologically debilitating. Her experience had led her to refuse to circumcise their three daughters. Picking up on this thread, a man now spoke of refusing to circumcise his daughter as an outgrowth of his own suffering from his wife's sexual passivity and fear of intimacy.

Then Mohammed spoke. A father of three girls, he circumcised his oldest daughter, resulting in the loss of her trust and love. Now he adamantly rejected the practice for his younger daughters.

Several attributed their escape from circumcision to the intervention of an older sister. Maiaka talked to her mother about the shame and horror of being exposed to a stranger's eyes, her deep sense of betrayal, and in the aftermath, a sense of worthlessness. Her mother was persuaded to spare her younger sister.

Omar held the group in rapt attention as he related how his conversation with a member of the group had changed his life. He had four daughters, but only the two eldest were circumcised. His second nearly bled to death after her circumcision, so he did not circumcise his third and fourth, even though he knew it might bring condemnation from family and neighbors. "For the last five years," Omar confessed, "I have not been able to sleep, thinking I made the wrong decision. Then you came to my house and listened to my story. You told me I had done a good deed. This was a great blessing. I did the right thing! Now I can talk to other men in my village and tell them not to circumcise their daughters. I say to them: 'Look at me! I have four daughters. All, as you well know, are good and virtuous girls. Two are circumcised and two are not. The only difference between them is two I badly hurt and the other two I saved.'"

Profound and surprising, the greatest impact of the conversations of the past six weeks was on the group members themselves. Yes, the telling of stories had a cathartic effect on the storytellers. But it had a powerful effect on the listeners as well. Many drew resolve from the testimony and were emboldened to advocate.

On returning to her village from the meeting at the monastery, Khira collected the dozen girls who had been circumcised on that same fateful day. She related what she had learned. The same girl who could not raise her eyes or speak during the first days at the monastery meeting now urged her friends to join their voices with hers. "Remember what happened to us.

Remember the pain, the bleeding, the shame." Her friends, avoiding eye contact, conveyed assent. They winced in the reliving of these memories. "Should we let this happen to our sisters?" Khira asked. The girls shook their heads vigorously. "This tradition must stop," she proclaimed. "Let us go and tell our mothers." And they did.

Women at the Well

At first glance, the scene at the well, a lively tableau where conservatively dressed old women and young girls swirling in long flowering dresses mixed and mingled, was the same as it had always been. For thousands of years, in hundreds of villages across Egypt, women of all ages have gathered at wells just like this to collect water for household chores, to gossip and laugh, to share joy and hardship. But on this day, one thing was different. Khira, the sixteen-year-old unschooled local girl who had recently gone outside the village for the first time in her life to attend a three-day meeting, carried herself differently. She was among the community activists who had gathered together to discuss the topic of FGM.

"The body is the same, her bearing is different," an old woman whispered to companions as Khira approached the well. As the young girl drew closer, she said: "You are different, Khira. Your eyes have been opened. Your ears have been opened. You talk about big things."

Khira responded, unembarrassed: "Not my ears, not my eyes, but something bigger. It is my mind. It was dark and closed, and now it is opened and sees the light."

Following the monastery workshops, the movement continued to flow forth. Efforts were catalyzed through support networks that built and sustained momentum. Ensuing initiatives combined volunteers, PDs, and NGO staff. Over succeeding weeks, local participants reported successfully convincing at least one community or family member not to circumcise their preadolescent girls. Of eight communities participating in the now expanded project, two report that not a single girl was circumcised during the traditional FGM season the following year.

Aftermath

In February 2004 we returned to Egypt to find out what had happened in the five years since we left. It was cold, unusual for Cairo at that time of year. I was prepared to be disappointed, anticipating that five years on, the seeds sown would lie fallow or have mutated into something bearing little resemblance to original intentions. My notes capture an account of an outcome that was quite the opposite:

> I was totally unprepared for what we have witnessed over the past five days in the field. The government is running a Female Genital Mutilation Abandonment program (FGMA) in three new governorates in Upper Egypt (Quena, Assiut, and Minya). The initiative is supported by Unicef. An Egyptian study published in 2000 had shown that FGM prevalence had dropped to ninety-three percent, down four percent in a three-year period. An idea whose time has come?
>
> Old and young men are here, the sheikhs with their turbans and voices of authority, doctors in suits and ties, farmers in their djellabas. Proud tales of triumph over nearly impossible odds. Women are here too, all ages, a sea of faces—wrinkled, weathered, youthful and bright, a mosaic of old and young. Some are partially or completely veiled, others unshrouded. Men and women sit together side by side! The women do not whisper or hesitate as they speak. It is happening. What began in the monastery has born fruit.

This promising use of the PD approach has endured the test of time. It has resulted in thousands of confirmed averted circumcisions in dozens of "FGM-free" villages, and in breaking the code of silence surrounding the subject. This application of the PD process has given a voice to the silenced girls and opponents of the practice from every walk of life. Most important, it has provided an empowering new perspective on the capacity of "people just like me" to change things.

As of 2007, the program had identified more than a thousand positive deviants and had spread to 1,693 families in some forty communities working with twenty local NGOs in four governorates (provinces) in Egypt.[3] Through multitargeted and multichanneled initiatives (from mosques, schools, churches, informal women's and men's groups, hospitals, etc.) sponsored by newly formed, constantly evolving formal and informal networks of advocates, villagers have "social proof" that it is possible to be uncircumcised and still be a "virtuous woman." Evidence that "someone just like me" has abandoned the practice provides tradition-bound villagers with an opportunity to break away from the practice. Monthly monitoring of "at-risk" girls in several villages has verified not only that thousands of circumcisions have been averted, but that PD has proven an exceptionally powerful tool. It has turned a near-universally perceived "intractable problem" into one whose solution exists in every village. The solution is just waiting to be uncovered and amplified.

For Khira, too, life goes on. She is now married and has a baby girl. She still receives an occasional taunt from village boys as she goes about her life. But she holds her head high. She travels to other villages working as an advocate for the cessation of FGM. Her daughter will be spared. She will never experience the trauma of Il Rittan.

Reflections

Trusting the process and the people made this happen, and this requires a profound shift in the traditional role of an NGO staff person. As an educated outsider, I had to let go of knowing it all, or indeed, of knowing anything. I had to surrender to the truth—anathema to educated "experts"—that listening is more powerful than speaking, asking questions more powerful than knowing. I had to let go of my fears and trust that others would deliver ideas and actions that were far beyond what I could dream or imagine. I was privileged to have been part of an epic of sorts, where ordinary people, through quiet acts of courage, stepped forward. Their voices were finally heard.

Success of the positive deviance approach is predicated on the principle that *telling* people about a new behavior or tool or strategy is not enough. People have to actually practice in order to internalize things and see the benefits for themselves. But how does that translate to this case of FGM? You can't practice *not* circumcising someone! The challenge was to find arguments, stories, and messages that were effective in convincing key decision makers—fathers, grandmothers, local religious leaders, and others with influence—to oppose FGM. Once captured, those stories weren't printed on pamphlets for distribution, enlarged into colorful posters, or pronounced over the radio as part of a public health campaign. Instead, cloistered in that windswept monastery, those first volunteers *practiced* reciting the stories, role-played how they would discuss this sensitive issue with community members, and shared their own stories with one another. They *practiced* the deviant behavior of speaking out, gaining trust, and breaking a taboo. Once they began speaking with others, the practice of speaking out took on a life of its own and began to spread. Emboldened by the growing acceptance and validation of their beliefs and actions, many PDs made the leap from silent dissenters to vocal community leaders. They have become not only frontline soldiers for curtailment of FGM, but also a force behind women's advocacy in Egypt. Initial tokens became effective minorities. Gradually the old orthodoxies gave way.

Curtailment of FGM is a problem for which no technical remedies are possible. Progress required shifts in norms and social acceptance. There were no tangible fixes such as the addition of shrimps, crabs, and greens to a Vietnamese child's diet. Success or failure turned entirely around making private conversations public, allowing the community at large to square perceptions with realities, norms with their consequences on young girls' lives.

FGM is the poster child for a problem enmeshed in social complexity and requiring behavioral change. It sheds light on the often underappreciated truth that *learning and change take place in a social context.* The power of the positive deviance process to crack the most intractable of problems derives from its embrace of the social system from the onset, seeing it not as a barrier to the implementation of somebody else's solution but as the means to a community's indigenous solution.

Psychologist Jerome Bruner juxtaposes "learning about" (primarily based on intellect) versus "learning to be," which shapes identity (and is informed by and anchored in a social system).[4] "Learning to be" creeps up on us through social interactions and practice—not cognition. Cessation patterns of cigarette smokers are a case in point. Despite admonishments regarding cancer, ostracism in restaurants, and nicotine patches, only one-third who try to quit alone succeed. When smokers become part of a support system, two-thirds succeed.[5]

Social Proof

A well-known principle of chemistry establishes that two active ingredients can be mixed together with little effect until a third ingredient—often an innocuous catalyst—triggers a chemical synthesis. Analogously, the social system is the catalyst between all that stuff we "know" versus what actually alters our behavior and mental maps.

Social proof?[6] Simple idea, really: it boils down to "seeing is believing." When someone "just like me" does something, I'm much more likely to do it myself. In Egypt, social proof was both enemy and ally. Social proof had held FGM in place since the pharaohs. And social proof was becoming the key to FGM's undoing.

Consider canned laughter. According to Cialdini, audiences say they dislike it, yet it is widely employed in TV and radio, notwithstanding well-documented objections. Why does the media ignore audience sentiment? Because laugh tracks evoke louder and longer laughter. More remarkable still, canned laughter has its biggest effect when the humorous material is of poor quality! Laughing because others are laughing testifies to the power of social proof. It provides us with shortcuts as to how to behave. It can also be exploited. (Why do you think Starbucks baristas prime their tip jars with $1 bills from their own pockets?)[7]

Social proof is especially important under conditions of uncertainty when we rely on others to guide us. Imitation is our fallback when reason doesn't suffice. This is true for situations from the trivial to the profound. Cialdini observes that we use social proof to decide how to dispose of an empty popcorn box in a movie theater, how fast to drive on a highway, or whether to tackle that fried chicken or corn on the cob with our hands at a dinner party. At the more consequential end of the spectrum, we rely on social proof to inform moral choices—whether to assist an inebriated football enthusiast who falls on the sidewalk or to step forward as a whistle-blower and call attention to illegal or inappropriate conduct.

In Egypt, social proof was the scimitar that cut both ways. The PD process juxtaposed old orthodoxies with data on the unconventional. It opened the eyes, ears, and consciousness of the community to new possibilities. It revised beliefs through practice. Essential in all this was diversity of opinion, independence of thought, and decentralization of authority such that stakeholders from all levels could discover and own the answer.

Preconditions for Innovation

Evolutionary biology teaches us that prolonged periods of equilibrium yield comparatively little change. Then comes a meteor impact or a volcanic event that enshrouds the sun, cools the earth, and alters life significantly.

Referred to as punctuated equilibrium, the most notable example is the Cambrian era commencing 542 million years ago, which ushered in the precursors to almost every species with seed or stamen, eye or antenna, foot or fin, that has inhabited the planet since.

The PD process gives rise to punctuated evolution in human time scales. Over human history there are many examples of remarkable innovations spawned in the direst of circumstances. A fundamental premise of PD is that in the most impossible of circumstances, usually someone, somewhere, has figured out a way to cope. While the wider community may believe "this will not budge" or "that's just the way it is," contrarian PDs seem to be as challenged by the "impossible" as Himalayan mountaineers are by unascended summits.

However, in nature generally and human systems specifically, crucial elements are sufficient diversity and social leeway to allow for individual experimentation in the first place and a disruption of homeostasis to allow for broader adaptation. Creativity can manifest itself boldly in the face of physical obstacles. But the straitjacket of social conformity can suppress experimentation altogether. The antidote is, to repeat, diversity, which for our purposes is best fostered by inclusion. Many problems seem intractable precisely because the conventional wisdom surrounding them is reinforced (and compounded) by a closed and limited circle of stakeholders whose minds are already made up. In the FGM experience, the expanded definition of positive deviants included not only girls who had not been circumcised but also the decision makers and authorities in their lives who had resisted tradition to curtail the practice.

Human beings can respond to high levels of disequilibrium in reactive ways. They may hunker down and reject the disruptive variant. Unsurprisingly, over the course of history from Plato to Galileo forward, many innovators have evoked a hostile reception when insight upended the entire order of things. The positive deviance approach attempts to lower the barriers imposed by social conformity and diffuse the shock effect by separating innovation as an outcome from the architecture of discovery. Specifically, job one is to mobilize the community's curiosity such that it is in search of alternative solutions (rather than surprised by and reflexively resistant to them). Because positive variants *already coexist* in harmony with the community that encompasses them, this disarming presence often bridges the gulf of incredulity.

We turn now to observe the potency of this framework in the buttoned-down and change-resistant universe of institutional medicine.

FOUR

Hospital Infections

Acting into a New Way of Thinking

In 2006, the Veterans Administration hospital in Pittsburgh, Pennsylvania, having exhausted all other methods to curtail the transmission rates of MRSA (an extremely dangerous hospital-cultivated bacteria), turned to the positive deviance approach. Jerry found himself at the frontier in applying PD in the most organizationally complex setting in which the approach had ever been undertaken. His account captures events as they unfolded and the adaptations necessary to tailor PD to this unique environment.[1]

IN 1847, DR. IGNAZ SEMMELWEIS, a Hungarian physician working in a hospital in Vienna, discovered a staggering discrepancy between maternal mortality rates in two wards of the hospital. Semmelweis noticed that deaths from fever connected to women in childbirth were much more numerous among women attended by doctors and medical students than among women attended by midwives.[2]

---

*The following story of the application of PD to eliminate hospital-acquired MRSA focuses primarily on the Veterans Administration Pittsburgh Health Service (VAPHS). As the initiative has spread from the VAPHS beta site to additional hospitals, project design and implementation has undergone many refinements. For the sake of readability, the hospital location of anecdotes and design refinements is not mentioned in the story. While all the data and anecdotes in this chapter are factual, they are a composite of the PD initiative in multiple hospitals, rather than strictly limited to events at VAPHS.

The doctor's research led him to the discovery that fatal infections were spread among patients by doctors who failed to wash their hands between examinations. Unlike the midwives, whose practice was restricted to attending relatively healthy pregnant women in their ward, medical students and doctors routinely examined their female patients upon returning from the morgue, where they performed autopsies on diseased cadavers. (In the mid-nineteenth century it was common for a doctor to move directly from one patient to the next without washing his hands, or to move from performing an autopsy on a diseased body to examining a living one.)

Semmelweis immediately instituted a procedure requiring physicians to wash hands with chlorinated lime solution between patient visits as well as to change into clean lab coats before examining patients. As a result, hospital mortality rates from infectious diseases declined dramatically.

One hundred sixty years later, more than nineteen thousand Americans die every year from hospital-acquired infections such as methicillin-resistant Staphylococcus aureus (MRSA), and one hundred thousand more acquire significant enough exposure to the MRSA bug to extend their stay in the hospital.[3] MRSA is caused by skin-to-skin contact as well as by contact with shared personal items or equipment. That benign grey and black silk necktie the surgeon is wearing on his rounds can be a potent vector of transmission, as can the blood pressure cuff that a few minutes ago was on the arm of the patient in the adjoining room with a surgical site infection. Although completely avoidable through diligence, the potential number of vectors and opportunities for transmission are staggering.

Erin's Story

Erin, an attractive forty-year-old registered nurse, seemed small and vulnerable. She stood before a crowd of a hundred-plus to kick off the MRSA Prevention Initiative. Largely eclipsed by the podium, she spoke in a quiet monotone, conveying detachment as if she were telling someone else's story.

"When I noticed a boil on my thirteen-year-old son's thigh, I waited a few days before I took him to the doctor, who incised and drained it, and then sent us home with a prescription for an antibiotic. We filled the prescription, but a few days later the doctor called and said he wanted to change the antibiotic. I didn't think anything of it at the time, and so I promptly filled the new order. But a few weeks later another boil appeared, and the doc once again lanced and drained it. As a nurse, I was able to care for my son at home, changing his dressings as needed, but with no exceptional vigilance.

"While all this was going on, my husband was preparing to undergo spinal surgery for a longstanding back problem. Soon after the surgery he developed a severe infection, which tested positive for MRSA. We were devastated, but had to carry on. What followed were multiple intravenous courses of powerful antibiotics." Now tears began to form in the corners of Erin's eyes, defying her apparent calm. "My husband had to endure four additional surgeries to deal with the infection," she continued. "He went through months and months of terrible pain and suffering from the side effects of the treatment. I became haunted with the prospect that perhaps I was somehow responsible for spreading MRSA from my son to my husband."

Control cracking, voice betraying grief and guilt, Erin willed herself to continue. "Sometime later when I was working in the maternity unit, I noticed a small infection on my neck. You got it," she said, staring blankly ahead. "It was MRSA! My husband was on his back for six months, unable to get up, unable to go to the bathroom, so depressed, so depressed . . . " Her voice was now barely audible: "so depressed." Erin took a very deep breath, making eye contact with the audience for the first time. "It finally ended when . . . when he took his life."

The deadly consequences of the knowledge–practice gap, personified in the story Erin told, was precisely what Dr. Jon Lloyd wanted to talk about one March morning in 2005. Dr. Lloyd, a retired general and vascular surgeon, was a man with a mission. He had been asked by the Centers for Disease Control (CDC) to work out of VAPHS to spearhead an effort to reduce MRSA at a consortium of forty-two hospitals in western Pennsylvania. Dr. Lloyd's challenge was to tackle an endemic condition widely regarded as inevitable in the hospital environment.

Simulations That Bite

An improvisation exercise vividly portrays the ease and speed at which MRSA can spread. A group of hospital staff are playing the roles of an infected MRSA patient and those she comes in contact with over a thirty-minute period.

The "patient," a fifteen-year-old girl named Rose, is lying in her bed with an irregularly shaped five-inch patch of chocolate pudding (representing the MRSA infection site) on her leg. Although in reality the wound would be covered, it still represents a potential transmission site, as some of the staph bacteria may be present on the dressing. Her hand periodically scratches the infection site, just as one's tongue might continually explore a painful tooth. Soon, several of Rose's fingers are covered with chocolate pudding. She scratches her forehead and a small patch of chocolate pudding appears at the hairline. Rose's mother, sitting on a chair at bedside, tenderly caresses her daughter's hair. Traces of chocolate pudding (surrogate for the actual MRSA bacteria) are now clearly visible on her hands.

A nurse comes into the room to check on Rose. Her mother gets up to shake hands and introduce herself. The nurse now joins the club; a trace of chocolate pudding, certifying her membership, clearly visible on her palm. Without washing her hands the nurse examines Rose, and adds further chocolate stains all over the patient, her bed, and the bedside table on which she places her stethoscope. Over the next minutes of this time-accelerated role play, a realistic number of other hospital staff, including a doctor, cafeteria staff delivering Rose's lunch, and a technician drawing a blood sample, enter the room. A few of them use the hand gel machine on

Rose's wall when they enter the room but forget to use it when leaving. They are now visible MRSA/pudding transmitters.

Hospital staff observing the role play cannot help but laugh at the dark humor. The bed, bedside table, chair, telephone, and all the actors are stained with chocolate pudding. Unfortunately, the reality is no laughing matter. The humorous improvisation captures the enormity of the challenge facing hospitals in attempts to eliminate preventable annual deaths and MRSA transmission. The bug respects no hospital hierarchy or the precautionary posters on hospital bulletin boards. Elimination requires nothing short of 100 percent compliance to the same hand-hygiene protocols outlined by Semmelweis in 1847.

Several countries in northern Europe—notably, Denmark, Finland, and the Netherlands—have virtually eliminated the bug.[4] Meanwhile, incidence of MRSA soared from 2 percent to 65 percent in the intensive care units of U.S. hospitals between 1995 and 2005.[5] Its reach grows every year. Ask about the problem next time you visit a hospital. Most doctors and nurses shrug their shoulders and respond, "Well, we're a hospital. It goes with the territory." That tends to be the end of the conversation.

Hospital-acquired bugs are almost unstoppable precisely because the bacteria are cultivated in a hazardous environment. It is a turbocharged version of natural selection. The organism learns to adapt in *almost* sterile conditions where drugs employed to kill the invader are constant adversaries. But given one single breach of precautions, the bacterium can mutate its way through the gauntlet of mankind's defenses, morphing into a "superbug" in the process.

The evidence-based protocol to kill these bugs before they take hold is widely disseminated among hospital personnel: thorough hand hygiene, appropriate gowning and gloving, and active surveillance. Procedures are drilled into every medical student, nurse, and orderly. Yearly classes are required for recertification to ensure familiarity with essential precautions. All hospital employees periodically affix their signature to a statement of compliance. Yet studies of U.S. hospitals from 1994 to 2000 indicate that adherence to appropriate hand hygiene is between 29 percent and 48 percent.[6] When you enter a hospital today for *any* reason (including just as a visitor), your encounter with the facility and its health care team constitutes a sort of Russian roulette in which the bacterium is the bullet and the hospital is the gun.

The limitations of the standard model, touched upon briefly in chapter 1, were increasingly self-evident to Dr. Lloyd. Reliance on top-down dictates and command-and-control solutions had utterly failed to control (let alone eliminate) MRSA. True, the "technical" procedures, *if properly followed* (e.g., annual trainings, ubiquitous hand washing, posters, and signatories of compliance), should do the trick. But these measures relied upon "thinking one's way into a new way of acting." The Achilles heel of it all lay in the phase *properly followed*. The problem persisted because of the hospital's complex social system. This encompassed a well-delineated status-sphere extending from surgeons to low-paid orderlies, cleaners, and service personnel and through the subcultures of proud medical departments (e.g., pediatrics, radiology, anesthesiology, orthopedics). Between silos and within the hierarchies of each, alignment on a strategy to eliminate MRSA seemed a bridge too far. Behavioral change (not just cognitive awareness) was essential to make significant progress.

Two wards in the acute care facility of the VA Pittsburgh Healthcare System had virtually eliminated the bug. To achieve this formidable feat, the hospital had employed the Toyota Production System (TPS), a very effective but expert-intensive industrial model that required a designated expert problem solver and a TPS teacher for each ward. Two wards proved that it was possible within the constraints of the Pittsburgh VA hospital to curtail MRSA transmissions. But after four years of implementation, identified solutions still had not spread to other units. Lack of uptake is the crazy-making paradox at VAPHS as well as other health care facilities throughout the U.S. Health care providers *know* what to do, but the large throughout the U.S. Health care providers *know* what to do, but the large number of Americans who die of hospital-acquired infections offer tragic testimony that they are not doing it.

Remedy of Last Resort?

If a doctor recommends daily exercise to raise your heart rate, it would be overkill to train for a triathlon. While the PD process is not nearly as onerous as the analogy suggests, there is a grain of truth in the hyperbole. It takes time. It requires the mobilization of a significant proportion of the affected community.

The positive deviance approach is a specialized tool for particularly intractable problems. Appropriately, one turns to it when other approaches have failed and other alternatives are exhausted. Through a process of elimination, technical solutions and top-down programs (e.g., the Centers for Disease Control's protocol to curtail MRSA, Pittsburgh's isolated pockets of success with the Toyota Production System) bring sponsors to the point where resignation sets in. Alternatively, sponsors cast about for something totally different. That's usually when the PD approach attracts attention. That's why Dr. Lloyd made the phone call.

VAPHS was not wrong to try other things before turning to "the remedy of last resort." The Toyota Production System used at the Pittsburgh VA (and its derivatives, Six Sigma and Lean) have much in common with the PD process—at least in concept. One of the authors, Richard Pascale, launched his academic career with an in-depth look at Japanese management.[7] Paradoxically, both then (the 1970s) and now, Japanese manufacturers such as Toyota, Honda, Sony, and Panasonic welcomed competitors to tour their plants and study their methods. When asked about the risks of sharing trade secrets with competitors, their answer (greatly abbreviated) was the same: "The visitors only focus on the *what*. They either overlook or are culturally incapable of grasping the *how*." Sounds familiar.

Toyota's culminating insight wasn't Kaizen, the "Five Whys," or its disciplined use of statistical quality control to improve production flow. Rather, it used these protocols to transform an assembly line into a continuous learning system. This entailed a top-to-bottom revolution in corporate culture. It reversed the flow of influence and authority in favor of the shop floor and quite literally turned the corporate pyramid on its head. Assembly line workers now occupy the *top* of the learning pyramid. Experts, industrial engineers, functional heads, and senior managers serve an enabling role in the never-ending quest for perfection. Plainly put, these organizational attributes bear little resemblance to the culture of most hospitals and corporations.

Given sufficient time, funding, technical expertise, and the right circumstances, organizations can, and do, get processes like Lean, Six Sigma, and TPS to work. TPS is credited with reducing MRSA transmission in two wards of the hospital. But transplanting the TPS approach or other best practices from greenhouse to jungle often fails. More often than not, the celebrated solution is greeted with cries of "not invented here" and "we're not them." (Defensiveness is guaranteed when the best practice is interpreted as code for "Why aren't you as good as the other guy?") Onlookers discount advocates for having incubated success under exceptional and unreplicable conditions. The processes often rely on top-down or outside-in authority, not on the community itself, to identify and introduce a superior template. When identification of a superior method is imposed and not self-discovered, voices charging exceptionalism limit uptake.

As we would witness in Pittsburgh, the PD process focuses on the *how*; alternative methodologies focus more on the *what* (e.g., the solution for malnutrition in Vietnamese villages was not just the *what* of shrimps, crabs, and greens but the *how* of persuading caregivers to feed their children nontraditional foods and the *how* of developing new habits of collecting these ingredients and feeding children more often).

There are also differences between the Toyota approach and the positive deviance process.[8] While both are grassroots, inquiry-driven methods that rely on facts to determine common practices and outcomes, the application of the Toyota process is generally confined to continuous, repetitive activities, not the one-off, idiosyncratic, and amorphous processes for which PD is well suited. The Toyota Production System and its incarnations capture many of its breakthroughs from bottom-up identification of non-value-added work. PD draws its inspiration from preexisting variants who have already succeeded in finding a better way.

While both PD and TPS tackle problems embedded in culture and social systems (and both may result in behavioral change), the PD process *insists* on the precondition that the community determine whether it wants to tackle the change in the first place. Members can opt in or opt out. The TPS methodology invariably arises when management decides to do a Lean or Six Sigma program. As with PD, orientations are held to acquaint workers with the technique. This can entail simulations to break the ice and draw attention to non-value-added work. In the best of circumstances, employees volunteer to engage in the process (and, in this respect, can opt in or opt out). So far, so good, except in most industrial settings this volunteerism is coerced. The acid test of whether those in authority or those in the community own the initiative is whether it is self-sustaining after extra resources and pressure to engage are withdrawn.

Unfortunately, the drift in most Western organizations is such that the practices tend to atrophy once management turns its attention to the next new thing. As contrasted to in Vietnam and Egypt, this has not been the case there. New habits were internalized in perpetuity because the community owned the choice to discover them.

The Positive Deviance Process Meets Goliath

Dr. Lloyd was on the phone the same day he read the article on PD. "You've got to help us," he began. "For four years I've been on a jihad with hospital staff to practice the protocols which have been so effective in Four West [one of the wards at VAPHS that had eliminated MRSA]. I've invited the other forty-one hospitals in the Western Pennsylvania Consortium to replicate our success. They come, they see, they 'learn,' then they go back to their units and not a hell of a lot happens!"

The frustration in Dr. Lloyd's voice reflected his incredulity that people could know what needed to be done to save lives and limbs (amputation is one of the graver consequences of some MRSA infections), yet they just weren't doing it. The challenge here was not to discover *what* to do, but *how* to get people to actually do it. Reading about the PD approach, Dr. Lloyd intuitively sensed that there might be a better way to bridge that gap.

We began working with Dr. Lloyd a month later. The chemistry was immediate and we bonded from the start (not a PD prerequisite, but nice when it happens). Dr. Lloyd, it turned out, had spent twelve months in Vietnam in the early '70s, when he served as an army surgeon. Not only did we have Vietnam in common (though in radically different circumstances), but he loved Brahms and the Marx brothers, and was somewhat irreverent about all institutions, be they his Mormon faith or the exalted status of surgeons.

Dr. Rajiv Jain, chief of staff at the Pittsburgh VA, created a core team composed of key hospital stakeholders (director of infectious disease prevention, director of nursing, infection control nurses, data analysts, and Dr. Lloyd). Dr. Jain sent invitations to everyone in the hospital to meet and learn about a new approach, PD, "which might be of interest." "Everyone" included people from housekeeping, transport, the pharmacy, the kitchen, and the lab. One imperative of the PD approach is to reach beyond the "usual suspects" and include representatives from the whole system. Success requires ownership from everyone whose behavior or practices might need to change. Those in any way implicated with the problem are a vital part of its potential solution.

The first meeting began with a presentation by the director of infection control using pie charts and data to illustrate the enormity of the MRSA problem. Abstract numbers were supplemented by personal stories such as Erin's. Stories put a human face on MRSA's toll. Our part was to provide examples from the developing world to illustrate the application of PD to a variety of problems such as female circumcision, girl trafficking, malnutrition, and HIV/AIDS risk reduction. As was essential, the ninety-minute session ended with an invitation and call to arms from the chief medical officer: "Anyone who thinks PD could be a useful approach to eliminate MRSA infections here at the hospital, and wants to be part of that effort, meet us here tomorrow morning at 8 a.m. to figure out the next steps." The next morning, out of the hundred-plus attending the kickoff presentation, about forty nurses, doctors, cleaners, lab technicians, orderlies, clergy, pharmacists, and others showed up to form what became the core PD MRSA team.[9]

Over the first few months, members of the core team at VAPHS conducted group meetings with over four hundred hospital staff. Nurse Heidi Walker, one of the original core team members, wanted to make sure these sessions really grabbed the staff members' attention. Heidi had a brilliant idea. She set off for Costco and purchased the biggest box of macaroni she could find. Neighborhood kids helped her count the pieces in the outlet's Family Size Super Pack: 3,250! Back at the supermarket, she purchased an additional thirty boxes to reach the needed one hundred thousand pieces.

Heidi now displayed the macaroni in an enormous transparent container to illustrate the number of patients needlessly infected each year in the United States from hospital-acquired infections. Each of the forty focus group discussion sessions began with Heidi entering the room with the gurney and its macaroni-filled container. Lifting, then dropping, handful after handful of the pasta-as-patients onto the gurney mattress, she asked: "Do you know what this represents?"

The hospital staff was experiencing an important lesson in launching the PD process. Data needs to be dramatized, personified, and socialized. (For an illustration of crucial community buy-in, see "PD Tackles Dropout Rates in Argentina.") Whether in the form of chocolate pudding, as in the earlier transmission simulation, or macaroni, the community needs a

PD Tackles Dropout Rates in Argentina

"Socializing the data" saved the day in Argentina, where the PD pilot was about to go up in flames. The assignment seemed straightforward: could positive deviance lower staggeringly high dropout rates in elementary schools? While 86 percent of children in Argentina completed their elementary education, only 56 percent of children in the rural province of Misiones did.[a]

The session in Misiones Province, sponsored by the World Bank, brought together two dozen teachers and principals. The assembled were united in the suspicion that the Ministry of Education was trying to implicate them in high dropout rates and deflect attention from their own accountability for a woefully underfunded education system.

Imagine the setting: a stark cafeteria with concrete floors and folding steel chairs. The teachers and principals are seated, their arms folded across their chests. Body language speaks volumes: "Okay, dazzle us with your expertise. This problem involves a whole bunch of things we can't control. We're angry. We haven't been paid in six months. We don't want to be here." Blame for the dropout problem lay elsewhere: lazy students, uninterested parents, and lousy facilities.

Ten minutes into the introduction and halfway into the Vietnam nutrition program experience, an intense teacher with delicate features and striking red hair stabbed the air with her hand. Her animation signaled a challenge, not a question.

"Señor, Argentina no es Vietnam. Your approach will not work here! We haven't been paid in months. The parents of these children are worthless and disinterested and you, señor, know nothing of our situation or problems . . . "

"Señora, lo que tu dices es absolumente le verdad!" was the only authentic reply. "I know nothing of your situation. I have no solutions to your problem of high attrition. We are here today because some of you, sitting in this room at this very moment, already have the solution! Some of you have been able to retain over 85 percent of your students and overcome the significant barriers such as those you have just raised."

The assertion was reinforced by tables of data that provided dropout statistics for all 120 schools in the Misiones Province. (Make the problem concrete!) Working in small groups, the educators as "guru" found plenty of schools that clustered near the median. But they were utterly flabbergasted to discover that one school retained 100 percent of its pupils through sixth grade, and ten retained nearly 90 percent. How, they asked themselves, do these schools retain so many students? After all, their teachers presumably hadn't been paid either.

Over several hours arms across chests were gradually unfolded, unleashing expressive Latino voices in animated conversation. The focus shifted from fault and blame to what was going well, and what some of the very people in the room had been able to achieve despite the hardships they faced. This brought the group face to face with the fact that some schools, with the same resources and same constraints, were actually achieving impressive retention rates. Interest piqued; there was now a desire to understand what those schools were doing. Curiosity began to take precedence over the need to affirm their status as "victims." Before the session ended, the teachers and administrators were asked to decide whether the "*desviación positivo*" approach made any sense, and whether they wanted to try to apply it in their schools to address the retention problem. The answer was an emphatic *sí*.

At the end of the day, the head of the teachers' union anxiously took an informal poll to see what her colleagues thought of it all. Her conclusion: "I don't know what transpired today. But this is the first time in a long while that I have seen these people come out of a meeting not angry and blaming someone for something!"

The next morning a similar session was conducted with a group of twenty-two parents who had been driven to the meeting by some of the same teachers who had attended the workshop the day before. This reflected a major triumph in its own right. Discussion the previous day had surfaced reservations about parental involvement: "It will not be possible for us to bring parents here tomorrow as you propose. They are not interested!" (Unstated was initial reluctance to give up another day of personal time, to chauffeur poor, vehicle-less parents back to a useless meeting!) Apparently some teachers had a change of heart.

From the outset, the meeting with parents was much less hostile than the first hours of the teachers' meeting the previous day. The seventeen mothers and five fathers had been briefed by the now almost enthusiastic teachers. They had conveyed how important it was for the parents to attend. The parents, mostly first-generation Argentineans of Eastern European descent and a few indigenous Indians, were more than a little flattered to be invited to a meeting by the Ministry of Education. Mostly subsistence farmers, they had changed from simple field attire to their Sunday best.

The parents were accustomed to the disdain of the more educated and comparatively middle-class teachers and administrators. They had never before been invited to share their ideas. Immediately and intuitively, they responded to the positive deviance approach. Asked to discuss positive deviants they had known in their own lives, all had examples and many viewed themselves as PDs. They were eager to share how they were able to overcome some of the barriers that plagued their rural existence.

Here, as on many occasions in the past, one witnessed the readiness of those eking out existence on the margins of society, with neither privilege nor prospect, to grasp the simple elegance of the

PD approach—in contrast to the skeptical consideration of the more educated and/or privileged. Uptake seems in inverse proportion to prosperity, formal authority, years of schooling, and degrees hanging on walls.

The discussion with parents centered as it had the day before, on the extremely high dropout rate of students by the third grade. Not surprisingly, parents' identification of probable causes did not center on "disinterested parents," but on (1) the difficulties of working with teachers who were "unfriendly" and "condescending," (2) teachers who didn't care about their students, and (3) teachers who made clear that the parents were not welcome in the school.

Time for the conceptual somersault? "Do all teachers behave like this?" Answer: "No." Some are much more welcoming, concerned, and inclusive. By the end of the six-hour session, the parents also gave a reassuring *sí* in response to their interest in using PD to address their school issues.

Over the months that followed, teachers and parents from ten typical schools visited the high-retention schools and discovered the differentiating factor had little to do with what was happening in the classroom. What differed was that teachers in the more successful schools were negotiating annual "learning contracts" with each rural parent before the school year began. In effect, they were enrolling illiterate parents as partners in their children's education. As the children learned to read, add, and subtract, they could help their parents take advantage of government subsidies and compute the amount earned from crops or interest owed at the village store. With parents as partners, students showed up and did their homework. The teachers involved in the PD process subsequently began negotiating similar contracts with families of at-risk children in their own classrooms. One

year later, Misiones documented a 50 percent increase in primary
school retention in the two districts participating in the initiative.[b]

a. Lucia Dura and Arvind Singhal, "Will Ramon Finish Sixth Grade? Positive Deviance
for Student Retention in Rural Argentina," Positive Deviance Wisdom Series (Boston:
Tufts University Positive Deviance Initiative, 2009), 1–8; Elina Dabas and Debora Yanco,
Enfoque de Desviación Positiva en el Ámbito Educativo: Misiones, Argentina, 2002–2003,
unpublished report prepared for the World Bank.

b. Dabas and Yanco, *Enfoque de Desviación Positiva*, 64–68. The positive deviance
approach was successful in improving retention in the districts in which it was piloted.
The question becomes: why did the initiative stall after the beta test? Two answers have
been offered by those on the ground. First, the World Bank, which sponsored the endeavor, asserts that the administrative cost in funding this $20,000 project was as great
as if it were a $2 million grant. Staff members are measured for productivity, defined as
dollars moved per unit of overhead expense. On this basis (unrelated to actual impact),
PD was not cost effective. A second explanation derives from the internal logic of the Ar-
gentine Ministry of Education. Lukewarm from the start, they seemed to be going along
only to accommodate the World Bank's enthusiasm for the endeavor. "There's nothing
in it for the officials," a ministry employee confided over dinner. "While the teachers
haven't been paid for six months, be assured the officials are receiving their salaries." He
continued: "They are interested in patronage." Large $2 million to $10 million World
Bank grants involve capital expenditures and construction projects. Inevitably, funds are
siphoned off, either directly or as "brokerage fees" in exchange for jobs on the project.
A $20,000 positive deviance project eliminates all this. Most of the money goes toward
the transportation of teachers and parents. Accustomed to patronage, they are terrified
by the prospect of PD replacing the World Bank's traditional way of doing business.

format that brings abstractions to ground. The people who need to change
need to understand what the data means.

Macaroni worked! The simulation made abstract numbers real. Participants chimed in with stories of how MRSA had affected them in their
professional or personal lives. Heidi built upon this personal testimony
with questions that served to launch the PD MRSA initiative:

What do you know about MRSA?

What do you do to prevent patients under your care from getting
MRSA?

What are the barriers that keep you from doing it 100 percent of the time?

Do you know of anyone who has figured out strategies to overcome these challenges? If so, how?

Do you have any ideas about new strategies?

What would it take to implement them in this unit?

Who is willing to take the next steps?

Dr. Lloyd and Heidi abandoned their home life to spend nights at the hospital, meeting with shifts that were unable to participate in the dozens of daytime focus group conversations. Wearily leaving one focus group meeting at 3 a.m., they were accosted in the elevator by the staff of the dementia unit, who demanded, "How come you haven't met with us yet?"

Dr. Lloyd and Heidi Walker had made a conscious decision not to involve the dementia unit, as these patients wandered from room to room and couldn't remember or observe precautionary measures. Only now did they reluctantly consent to do so. An hour and a half later they left the "bonus meeting" exhausted but exhilarated. They had witnessed the tremendous enthusiasm of the dementia unit staff and the buzz surrounding MRSA.

Over the following months, an ever-widening group of self-nominated volunteers joined the core team. The inquiry was beginning to ferret out colleagues who were actually doing something different regarding MRSA prevention: a doctor who ended each "patient round" with her staff in front of one of the gel dispensers located throughout the hospital, so she could use it (rather than talk about the importance of doing so). Another nurse had discovered (as the core team members would learn to their great chagrin) that the patients viewed the dispensers as the property of the staff and not for patient use, and she insured that all newly admitted patients knew it was theirs to use.

Latent Positive Deviance?

In addition to the existing, but uncommon, practices that were identified, some entirely new solutions began to emerge. Dr. Lloyd quickly comprehended and seized upon this important development. The PD process was not only tapping into existing uncommon practices, but also creating a climate of inquiry in which hospital staff could invent new solutions. Dr. Lloyd called this "latent positive deviance," the just-waiting-to-be-hatched solutions.

Latent solutions? Up to this juncture, our work in searching for positive deviants had focused on *preexisting* solutions. In this respect, positive deviance represents but one of many adaptive processes that mobilize a community to experiment and innovate. Now a larger possibility was in the offing. We had always been careful not to characterize PD as a "method" or "model," let alone a doctrine. There is a cogenerative symbiotic relationship between the PD process and the evolving social system. Surprising developments emerge as communities become engaged. The vector of dissemination for a PD discovery is this social virus. And true to the nature of all viruses, the PD process mutates. It was essential that the approach be malleable enough to adapt to the problem it was trying to tackle.

Latent solutions lay dormant in the hospital climate where conformity to evidence-based protocols, hierarchy, and silo-bound roles are the norm. With the disturbance of equilibrium brought about by the PD process, and with mechanisms in place to elicit and practice new ideas, a floodgate of potential solutions burst open. This is what natural scientists call "self-organization" and "emergence." Staff began to witness that their voices could be heard, and that their ideas had a good chance of being implemented. Uptake for their ideas came as a breath of fresh air against the backdrop of resignation that had arisen from previous attempts to control MRSA through regulation and enforcement. The social virus transformed a culture of resignation to one of innovation, from top-down edict to bottom-up experimentation and discovery. The hospital social system, once engaged, fostered curiosity and commitment that did not end when preexisting strategies for controlling MRSA had been exhausted. Viral experience morphed into a process of discovery and innovation.

Adaptations in Time and Space

In Vietnam and Egypt, daily rhythms and the pace of discourse in building relationships were comparatively relaxed. We could spend weeks talking with villagers about the issues and practices related to the problem at hand. A ninety-minute discussion with villagers, suffused by the smells of dried fish or chile peppers from the nearby outdoor market, or interrupted by the call to prayer at the local mosque, often provided a welcome diversion from the monotony of daily life. Mapping exercises with local leaders and villagers (using stones and twigs to represent children of the very poor who were not malnourished) turned out to be a stimulating experience. It could hold attention for hours. A half-day PD inquiry with a poor family with a well-nourished child or Egyptian families that had not circumcised their young daughters was often the high point in a day.

Hospitals are different! Notwithstanding the success of the initial orientation meeting on PD and successes over the first months of the hospital pilot, there was growing pushback that we could never get to scale "if it takes this much time." At a regularly scheduled "lessons learned" session, the head nurse of the orthopedics ward spoke for many in the room: "We like the approach, but it's just not possible to get people together for more than thirty to forty minutes, and certainly not more than once. Given the realities of this hospital and everyone's already overloaded schedules, there's no way you are going to get people to attend group sessions, then come up with indicators of success, identify positive deviants, go and interview them, and then meet to design opportunities for practicing those PD behaviors. Forget it."

To be scalable in a hospital setting, the PD approach needed an entirely new format, incorporating the requisite steps of identifying a candidate problem, allowing members of the relevant community to opt in or opt out, establishing a baseline of common practices through site visits and conversations among the stakeholders, and identifying existing PDs (or latent PDs). Somehow this had to occur within the strict limitations of the disciplined hospital clock.

With no idea on how to compress our four-week exploration into less than an hour, we went back to the VAPHS staff and asked them for their ideas. The result was the thirty- to forty-minute group discussion in which all these steps were explored at the same time. After several trials, the sessions morphed into action-oriented "discovery and action dialogues," or DADs. The DADs became the spark plug that ignited the PD engine. Other new forms emerged naturally, such as weekly stand-up briefings, "real-time" data-sharing mechanisms, and in-hospital MRSA Web sites and chat rooms.

Sessions would kick off with attention-getting MRSA transmission statistics. Participants would then try on blood pressure cuffs, remove gloves, and fold gowns, all to reveal how bacteria contaminate a sterile area. Then facilitators, previously self-selected from the ranks, would jump to the crucial question: "Is there anyone here who has overcome these challenges?"

Making Change Stick

Grasping that something momentous was unfolding, yet aware that the PD MRSA initiative could rapidly dissipate as the "flavor of the month," the core group sought to consolidate the beachheads of early success. Staff had seen many hospital campaigns ebb and flow. This time, making change stick could not be left to chance. Accordingly, ideas captured during the

DAD sessions needed to be acted upon immediately, and feedback loops confirming results achieved needed to reach every corner of the hospital. Changing the emphasis of the sessions from discovery to action had this effect. Facilitators drilled down when ideas surfaced. *"Great idea! What would it take to do that in this unit? Is there anyone who wants to volunteer to take those steps? Can you do it alone, or do you need help? Is there anyone who needs to be part of that decision who isn't here in this group now? How do we get her to the table?"* After a few tentative efforts, the facilitators mastered the "question as catalyst" technique. They came out of most sessions with milestones for future deliverables.

Evidence of action convinced people throughout the hospital that the PD initiative was not business as usual. The news spread rapidly. Elimination of MRSA became prominent in staff awareness. As mindfulness emerged, new solutions began to pop up in likely as well as unlikely places. Acting on these new practices quickly transformed initial discoveries into habit. This went a long way to sustaining the initial buzz.

Does the inclusion of "latent PD" blur the distinction between brainstorming, appreciative inquiry, and other participatory approaches? The simple answer is yes. But a fastidious or academic desire to differentiate the PD process must give way to pragmatic adaptation.

At the core, the distinguishing property of the PD approach is its focus on discovering positive variants in a community and mobilizing people to disseminate and integrate superior practices into the cultural DNA. PD interjects an internalization strategy into the traditional process of discovery. Clearly, reaching beyond preexisting variants and generating new approaches extend beyond the core concept. But essential aspects of the PD process (the community's and individual's decision to opt in or opt out, taking ownership of the process, investing sweat equity in mapping common practices and outcomes, discovering preexisting PDs, designing an action learning approach to spread discoveries to others) remain intact. Experience in Pittsburgh was taking on a life of its own. Ideas, previously held back, were put forward. Innovations became commonplace because people were paying more attention to the MRSA transmission problem and experiencing an idea-friendly climate, as the next four examples illustrate:

> Dr. Fred Chen, a reticent Hong Kong–born physiatrist, realized that both MRSA-infected and uninfected patients were using the same equipment without his department knowing who was who. This resulted in his request for a MRSA patient list and the creation of a new protocol for working with them and the equipment they used. This example captures how the PD focus on "solutions from within" leverages existing but underutilized resources. The patient list existed, but it never occurred to Dr. Chen that it might be of use to him in his work until the PD process set his sights on MRSA prevention. Learning that other staff ideas had been acted on gave Dr. Chen sufficient impetus to consider what he might do to eliminate MRSA in his own shop, clearly not a part of his job description.

> Tanis Smith is a gentle but physically imposing social services assistant, working with long-term-care patients at VAPHS. One of her responsibilities is to oversee weekly bingo games held in the recreation room. The bingo sessions are a high point of the week for many vets, providing an opportunity for some healthy testosterone-powered competition and a respite from time spent in their room or wheelchairs. The competition at the bingo sessions is pretty fierce. Occasionally, vets improve their odds of winning by bringing in an additional bingo card discreetly stashed in their socks or shorts.

> Shortly after the PD MRSA kickoff at VAPHS, Tanis reflected upon her routine. Following each bingo session, the vets were provided with a snack, but not with soap or alcohol rub to clean

their hands after handling the unsanitized bingo card. These guys were not only Tanis's patients; many were personal friends. The situation called for action. Tanis began carrying alcohol-based foam with her to every bingo session. Before the snack, she would approach each vet, ask for his hands, give a squirt and a smile and say, "Zap before you snack." The vets were more than compliant, and with the exception of one particularly macho guy who said he didn't need protection from anything, they gratefully accepted the foam and the concern. Soon this practice became the accepted norm at the bingo games. It is now as much a part of the routine as the calling out of letters and numbers.

The shuttle driver became aware that his vehicle, used to transport long-term patients to different facilities throughout the hospital system, was a potential MRSA infection transmission site. So he requested that soap dispensers be placed in the van. He, too, could "do something."

A MRSA awareness session with a diverse group of auxiliary hospital staff (dental hygienist, a few pharmacists, clerks, and a hospital pastor) soon made clear that basic knowledge about the hazard was very uneven. This prompted participants to become engaged in the infection transmission issue. After learning how MRSA can be spread by equipment and materials, as well as by direct hand contact, and how it can survive on some surfaces for as long as thirty days, the hospital pastor nearly leapt from his chair. "*My God!*" he shouted, "I'm probably spreading this thing all over the place, and all in God's name! I carry my bible from room to room, put it down next to the patient, and encourage him to leaf through it, then bring it into the next patient and start infecting all over again." That very afternoon the pastoral department introduced disposable bible covers, and God's emissaries began to gown and glove to ensure they were spreading nothing more than spiritual guidance.

The dementia ward staff who had waylaid Dr. Jon Lloyd and nurse Heidi Walker at the elevator demanding their own discovery and action session turned out to provide one of the most unlikely success stories. As noted earlier, Dr. Lloyd's initial decision to exclude the dementia ward was predicated on the seeming impossibility of their circumstances. Dementia patients sometimes share each other's clothes, occasionally even dentures. Soap dispensers can't be placed on walls without the risk of patients eating the contents.

The "conventional wisdom" about the dementia ward proved more conventional than wise. The first session with staff quickly shifted to discussing what some staff were *already* doing to overcome those barriers. One nurse, for instance, wore her own personal-size hand gel flask on her belt and used it to wash patients' hands before and after eating. This immediately became the common practice for other staff in the unit. Propelled by the PD focus on what is possible, other new ideas blossomed. These included special MRSA prevention and hand-hygiene training for families visiting dementia patients, provision of antibacterial towels for cleaning surfaces, and, most important, a belief that eliminating transmissions was indeed possible. The results have been extraordinary; "the most difficult unit for MRSA prevention" has turned into the most successful. After six months without a single transmission, a banner over the unit entry proudly proclaimed, "You are entering a MRSA-free zone!"

Epiphany at the CDC

"I was walking the hallway at Heinz [the long-term facility]," recounted Dr. Lloyd, "when Ted, a cafeteria employee, grabbed me by the shoulder and said, 'Dr. Lloyd, we've got a problem! I just noticed that despite the fact that we put tongs out next to the fried chicken, lots of folks just pick it up with their hands. There's no hand-hygiene dispenser in sight, and I'm really concerned that this might be an infection site. I've called a meeting of kitchen staff to discuss it this afternoon at four.'

"I shared this story the same afternoon with Dr. John Jernigan, our epidemiologist from the Centers for Disease Control (CDC)," Dr. Lloyd continued. "He was polite, but clearly unimpressed. 'Hands touching fried chicken are an unlikely MRSA transmission point,' he replied bluntly. As our infection control expert and CDC liaison on the PD MRSA initiative, I was aware that he was quite skeptical about PD. Given a choice between hard, evidence-based science versus the 'wisdom of the crowds,' he was unequivocal about where he would place his bets."

Six months later, after witnessing the results of staff passion and commitment to eliminate MRSA, Dr. Jernigan became a convert. One afternoon he reflected on his dismissive reaction to the food service's fried chicken–dispensing concerns. "CDC has developed uncontestable, evidence-based protocols to eliminate MRSA," he observed. "We issue them, reissue them, publicize and disseminate them. But it has taken PD to get people to actually act on them." With a characteristic mix of humor and humility, he added, "What a dummy I was. Whether or not the potential transmission site which Ted identified really constituted a significant risk or not is irrelevant. What *is* relevant is the collective mindfulness on the part of everyone at the hospital, regardless of role, about MRSA and their willingness to adopt new practices to combat it. Ted's concern about the tongs is a pretty good indicator that a lot of other people are getting scrupulous about hand-hygiene protocols as well."

Newton was right: every action has an equal and opposite reaction. The CDC's top-down solutions had mobilized countervailing forces. Reactions came in the form of avoidance, resistance, and exceptionalism. In contrast, when you fan the embers within a community rather than rely on firebrands from headquarters, change is self-propelled and natural. To shift the metaphor, internally developed solutions circumvent transplant rejection triggered by a solution deemed "foreign." Things go more smoothly when the change agents share the same DNA as the host. Group ownership confounds the immune defense response.

Beyond the Usual Suspects

The "usual suspects" for MRSA control at hospitals are management, infection control experts, doctors, and nursing supervisors. The DADs provided *everyone* at the hospital with an opportunity to act their way into a new way of thinking. They provided a catalyst for solutions from housekeepers, clergy, physical therapists, radiology—virtually every function and discipline in the hospital. One group had been curiously overlooked and fell way beyond the pale of "usual suspects": the patients themselves. So *patients* at VAPHS's long-term facility were invited to form their own volunteer group. They decided to evangelize other patients and their own families, outlining the hazards of MRSA and means of prevention. Of course, the hospital's infection control staff had published a brochure that attempted to communicate all this. But the patients wanted more edgy, in-your-face stuff. Their activism stood in stark contrast to the prevailing pattern of "passive recipient," the default setting for most patients in health care facilities.

We met Daryl, one of the prime movers of the initiative, during one of our visits to VAPHS. Daryl had contracted MRSA at the hospital. Resulting in an effort to stem the rapid spread of the infection, he had to endure several painful operations. If these proved unsuccessful, MRSA could well result in the loss of his leg. During weeks in recuperation, flat on his back in an isolation room, Daryl had nothing but time to contemplate his future and his present surroundings.

During a discovery and action session with other patients, Daryl told the following story. It resonated with fellow patients and left an indelible impression on nurses and doctors throughout the VAPHS long-term-care facility. "The alcohol hand-hygiene dispenser in my room was on the wall just behind my bed," he said. "That meant that I could never see if the doc or nurse coming in to see me was washing her hands or not. But, I got real good at *hearing* the slight 'squish' sound the dispenser made when it was being used. I would wait and pray that I would hear that squish before the doc or nurse came over and touched me! Lots of times though, there was silence, and I was scared. But there was one nurse who always used the dispenser before coming over to my bed. I was real happy whenever she came in the room and I knew I wasn't going to get a new bug."

Simple story. Strange how the squish of the hygiene dispenser could put an alert patient at ease. Subsequently, staff foreknowledge that "the patient might be listening" kept others on their toes. The "squish alert" served as a kind of conscience, having a more powerful impact on many in the facility than signs outlining proper hand hygiene ever could have. Knowledge that the thirty seconds it would take to use the dispenser might make the difference between a patient greeting the staff member with relief rather than dread was a profound impetus for behavior change.

Daryl's story also resulted in changing the placement of hand-hygiene dispensers to the wall facing the patient's bed (rather than behind it). The new placement not only empowered the patient to monitor health providers' hand hygiene, but (like those highway signs reminding you about speed surveillance with radar) staff became immediately and con-structively more self-conscious.

Drowning in Data, Thirsty for Relevance

Hospitals are data-intensive places. Earlier mention was made of the need to socialize and personalize data. Critical is not only the quality of the data but who owns it and how the owners use it. All units participating in the PD MRSA project report transmission and infection rates in com-pliance with an approved CDC protocol. Figures capture the number of nasal swabs inserted into so many nostrils, the number of transmissions of invisible staph bugs transferred from one surgical site or infected limb to another. These statistics are traditionally assembled like pieces of a mosaic and convey a meaningful picture to the quantitative-minded prevention control staff.

One nurse, on the other hand, was singularly unmoved by all this. The PD process enabled her to speak truth to power. Abstract and sterile, the reports made no human connections to her calling as a healer. At one of the periodic DADs, she voiced outspoken disinterest. Provoked, she rose from her chair, went to the wall where the transmission, surveillance, and infection charts were displayed, and challenged the group: "I know we have to collect these data and present to the CDC in this format. But what do those numbers really mean? What this chart says to me is that there are twelve people alive today, going to work, coming home and playing with their kids, who wouldn't have been alive if not for our efforts to control MRSA." Pointing to the second chart, she said, "There are another thirty-seven people who were able to go home and be with their families rather than remain here for an additional four weeks. We have to make the data human so the numbers speak to diligence or negligence." From that day forward, the same charts "spoke" differently to the unit staff as they passed them a dozen times each day.

A powerful point here. In Vietnam, caregivers could easily understand and grasp what the numbers meant (i.e., most of their children weren't "normal" for their age). Tracking showed when their children gained weight—a motivating factor for their continued practice of the new behaviors. In contrast, the CDC's data collection quest was viewed with indifference, serving the insatiable data needs of paper pushers. Overlooked but crucial stakeholders were left in the dark and unmotivated. Once these stakeholders created the context to *want* the data and recognized its relevance, the "foreign" language took on meaning.

One of the most powerful reinforcers of behavioral change is evidence that a newly acquired practice results in measurable improvement over the previous status. The people who need to change need to *own* these comparisons in order to "get" their relevance.

A noteworthy milestone along these lines (i.e., that the data is not "someone else's job") was the dramatic increase in swabbing *all* patients' nostrils at the time of admission, discharge, or transfer to a different unit. The nasal swab is cultured at the lab, and the results show whether the patient has MRSA or not. Because admission, transfer, and discharge are hectic, multitasking events (multiple forms must be filled out, releases signed, medication protocols verified), swabbing was chronically over-looked. Connecting the dots between these statistics and transmission triggered near-religious adherence to swabbing protocols. Even death was no excuse for nonadherence. (Discovering if MRSA is associated with any fatality is an essential element of a comprehensive statistical analysis.)

Dr. Lloyd explains: "I knew we were winning the share-of-mind battle when a nurse assistant ran out the hospital door, waving her arms at the hearse on its way to the mortuary. 'Stop, stop,' she panted, 'we forgot to do a nasal swab on the deceased!'" She missed the van, but not the opportu-nity to return to her ward to create a new fail-safe protocol. Working with a few of her colleagues and the supplies department, they taped nasal swabs to all the body bags. Today, the deceased's "final discharge" doesn't compromise 100 percent surveillance.

Tracking the use of soap and gowns turned out to be an effective lead indicator of MRSA mindfulness. Higher use signals a higher state of vigi-lance. An increase in gown use from three thousand a month prior to the PD MRSA initiative to its current monthly rate of twenty-four thousand suggests the scale of change afoot. Although laundering more gowns costs the hospital an additional $125,000 per month, it is more than offset by the estimated $35,000 cost savings associated with *each* MRSA case averted.[10] Over a six-month period at VAPHS, there were fifteen fewer MRSA surgical site infections than in a comparable period before the PD MRSA initiative—a savings of about $400,000 per month. This figure doesn't count the cost to the patients and their families of extended hospital stays and treatments, pain, suffering, and death.[11]

Results

Between July 2005, when the MRSA elimination initiative at VAPHS began, and October 2006, incidence of infection was reduced by more than 50 percent.[12] New dispensers are in place and, more importantly, in use throughout the hospital. Barrier precautions are being rigorously observed, and active surveillance of all patients upon entry and discharge is over 90 percent. Nurses, nurse assistants, cleaning staff, even patients now feel empowered enough to gently remind a remiss physician that he has forgotten to wash his hands. This would have been unthinkable a scant two years earlier.

"At our kickoff meeting in August of 2005," Dr. Lloyd observes, "had we asked a group of one hundred-plus hospital employees, 'Who in the room is responsible for infection control in the hospital?' they would have pointed to the four infection control staff. In October 2006, at a similar meeting at VAPHS, in response to the very same question, every hand in the room went up! MRSA control has become everyone's business. We've made so much more progress than before," Dr. Lloyd explains, "because we've shifted our emphasis from teaching people what to do, to engaging them as pioneers in discovering how to actually do it!"

Reflections

One of the often-cited drawbacks of the PD approach is the difficulty inherent in going to scale. Guilty as charged. Discoveries from one community cannot be repackaged and provided to another as a silver bullet. (That's a "best practice" rollout, and it invariably evokes the immune rejection response.)

Notwithstanding the hospital's clever adaptations to compress time, the PD process seems slower than what one might expect from top-down enforcement of hygiene protocols. The criticism is comparable to Winston Churchill's critique of democracy as "the worst form of government, except for all those other forms that have been tried from time to time." Admittedly somewhat slow and cumbersome, the PD process works because each community must own the choice to opt in or opt out. It works because, contrary to widespread faith in "communication" and "knowledge transfer," information has a social life, and unless new insights are embedded in the social system, they evaporate.[13] As the Centers for Disease Control personnel in the Pittsburgh VA were to discover, knowledge doesn't advance practice. Rather, practice advances (and internalizes) knowledge. After decades of reversals and rising MRSA statistics, staff and patients at the Pittsburgh VA were on the cusp of literally acting their way into a new way of thinking.

Within three years of the 2005 kickoff at VAPHS, the PD MRSA initiative has spread to more than forty hospitals and health care centers in the United States and Canada (and there is a pilot effort in Medellín, Colombia). Networks of hospitals have begun using the approach, and its application is growing exponentially. The VA hospital system, the largest in the United States, is currently piloting PD at an additional five beta sites. The entire 168-hospital system has been exposed to the approach. The state of Maryland, with the highest MRSA rates in the country, now has a growing consortium of hospitals using PD for MRSA elimination.

Here's the rub—the essential idiosyncratic nature of the PD approach thwarts the overeager in replicating it. But while self-discovery is critical to the PD process, *process* lessons learned in one setting *can* be shared and used in others to accelerate the initiative. (See "How Process Lessons Accelerate Progress.") Overall, what works best is something akin to the Living University as first discovered in Vietnam.

How Process Lessons Accelerate Progress

The VA's five beta sites illuminated process lessons that can accelerate learning. Initially, staff from fifteen candidate hospitals (including senior and middle management, infection control, and nursing and medical staff) came together for a day-long orientation on the PD approach and its applications to MRSA. At its conclusion, participants were advised of the financial implications, requisite staff time, and senior management support. Attendees returned to their hospitals and discussed the approach with their peers. Those assembled then decided whether they wanted to apply it in their location. This decision was not made by senior management; it was a joint decision of many MRSA-elimination stakeholders. This is essential to keep the ownership of the initiative where it belongs.

As mentioned, five of the VA hospitals elected to go ahead. Dissemination occurred through a network of PD consultant trainers who work directly with hospital teams. Lessons painstakingly learned over an eighteen-month period at VAPHS were shared during a three-day "training of PD facilitators" workshop. As appropriate, the takeaways were adopted at the new site. Process lessons pertained to issues such as the optimal time to begin carrying out DADs (immediately after the training), the categories of people to be invited to the kickoff (e.g., a cross section of everyone, rather than the usual suspects such as nurses and doctors), and the importance of feedback loops (essential). Noteworthy is that the *content* of these events was decided by each site, based on its own unique culture. This part can't be codified.

Borrowing from the Living University idea pioneered in Vietnam, the hospital core team members selected two or three units in their facility where they could pilot a PD Initiative in real time. These beta tests enabled them to perfect the specific kind of listening and facilitation peculiar to the PD process. They could invent their own chocolate pudding–type simulations that would spark interest within their respective communities. With external PD trainers observing, they tried their hand at a real workshop. The action learning–based pilots were then critiqued, additional skill training provided as needed, and off they went to do another workshop with another unit of the hospital. Result: within a few weeks, the VA's subsequent tranche of hospitals found themselves at the stage in the rollout that had taken the Pittsburgh beta site many months to achieve.

It became clear over time that although existing PD practices and new ideas were routinely discovered during the thirty- to forty-minute DAD sessions, often many were left to wither on the vine. Today, facilitators drill down and "capture" a good idea as soon as it is discovered, then translate it into action. "Catching butterflies" has emerged as a way to describe the process. It has become a part of the PD lexicon. "As soon as you see a butterfly, you need to take your net and capture it. It won't wait around until you've surveyed all the other butterflies." This gets into pretty tactical stuff, such as: Who will change the hand-hygiene signs in the room? When will they do it? Whose support or authorization is required?

Leveling the Hierarchy

Prior to the PD process, the supervising nurse of each VAPHS unit received a weekly "report card" from senior management. It measured how well that unit was performing. "Bad grades," metaphorically, meant being called to the "principal's office." The focus was always on what was going wrong—consistent with the blame culture of most large hospitals. The PD initiative turned the relationship between "prosecutor" and "defendant" on its head. Instead of having the unit heads receive data *from* manage-ment, the new protocol brings top management (the chief medical officer, director of infection control, etc.) to each unit for a monthly briefing from the unit staff.

Unit staff present *their* data for the preceding month to top manage-ment. The focus is now on what is going right. High swabbing rates and minimum transmission rates are celebrated. When transmissions occur, the entire unit team (not just the boss) presents an analysis of what might have caused the lapse and, more important, what actions are being taken to address it. The shift from being "exposed" by data presented *by* man-agement to analyzing, owning, and explaining it *to* management, has been transformative. What had previously been a punitive and fear-inducing experience has become a proactive, problem-solving process driven from the bottom up.

"You won't believe what just happened," Dr. Lloyd began his phone call to me in the fall of 2005. "I just came back from the briefing at the long-term care VA with Dr. Jain and the director of infection control. Eddy Yates, the housekeeper for the ward, presented the data to us! Not only did he go through all of the stats for the past month, he explained proba-ble cause of transmission for one patient reentering the unit. He was deeply involved in efforts to eliminate MRSA in his ward. He had full com-mand of the significance of the data, and had been chosen by his unit mates to present it to the hospital honchos!"

The PD MRSA initiative had not been designed to change the hospital culture. But a housekeeper presenting data to the chief of staff clearly indi-cated that's exactly what had happened. Eddy's story helped crystallize an insight that we have previously observed in passing. Cultural and social change, although not discrete objectives of PD interventions, are almost always a second-order outcome. Through addressing concrete, measurable, systemswide problems (such as MRSA elimination), relationships change, existing networks enlarge, power and authority become more widely shared, hierarchy flattens, and the quality, quantity, and nodes of communication proliferate and improve. And as a result, so does the culture.

Perhaps one of the most striking examples of culture change at VAPHS (and to varying degrees at the more than forty other hospitals and health care centers involved in PD MRSA elimination initiatives) is the shift in power relationships from a few designated leaders in the hospital organizational hierarchy to distribution throughout the entire informal network of staff and patients. Shared authority has enabled patients, janitors, and social services assistants to impact MRSA outcomes collectively and exponentially more effectively than a blizzard of top-down reminders from the CDC and the chief surgeon.

But shifting the flow of influence doesn't come easily, especially for those who may perceive themselves to be losing power and control: the CEO, chief medical officer, doctors, nurses, and especially the infection control personnel. Although *control* is one of two words in the latter job title, it comprises a much greater percentage of the identity of the "infection control" title holders. "Having the answer" is what years of training have prepared them to do. Furthermore, and most importantly, it is what they are being paid to do and the basis for their retention and promotion. If a problem arises that doesn't have a solution, it's their job to find one, and quickly. After all, lives are at stake. Absent a radical overhaul of job descriptions and mind-sets, expecting people in these positions to happily relinquish their role as prime problem solver, fixer, "expert," and decision maker is unrealistic. The whole enterprise can cause them to question their very raison d'être. Repeatedly, incumbents have reported the excruciating difficulty encountered when required to meet with a group of underlings and ask *them* for their ideas regarding solutions to MRSA-related problems.

Not providing the answer, when it was so evident, was described by one infection control officer as "more difficult than trying to stifle an oncoming sneeze. To take the extra few minutes to pose questions," he continued, "rather than provide the answer, took a lot of self-control and practice on my part. Only after did I begin to realize that the extra time I thought was being wasted in getting the staff to come up with the solution, actually translated into immediate uptake of *their* solution once they were discovered or created. Far from time wasted, it was saved. With PD," he concluded, "you go fast by going slow."

The Facilitator's Role

We were visiting with the PD core team at one of the beta site hospitals during the early implementation stage of their PD MRSA initiative. Several nurses passing in the opposite direction said, half jokingly, but with an edge in their humor, "Hey, here come the PD gestapo!" During a biweekly telephone conversation with another beta site, the PD core team sheepishly admitted to being referred to by some of their peers as the "PD nazis." Not exactly a desirable image for those meant to be nondirective *facilitators*.

The whole notion of creating an "authority-vacuum" to enable stakeholders to find solutions is the leitmotif of the PD facilitator's work. It is precisely because we knew nothing about hospitals when we began working at the VA in Pittsburgh that we were able to create the space for others to come up with solutions. Our *lack* of expertise regarding MRSA and hospitals created the vacuum that staff filled from the very beginning of "their program." It was easy for us not to provide solutions, because we didn't have any. It's much tougher for people with experience who *do* have answers to resist the impulse to provide them. In one of the beta site hospitals, the PD core team playfully decided to call their group the "tongue biters" in recognition of this difficult task!

Dr. Lloyd, in his endearing self-deprecating manner, told of his own struggle to relinquish his surgeon's deft but firm control of the helm in order to enable others to discover things: "When we first began our DADs," he began, with a shy grin, "we decided to video a session to demonstrate the process with other potential facilitators. When we reviewed the video, I was mortified. Every time I asked a question, if there was a pause of more than five seconds, I stepped in and gave the right answer! I was doing most of the talking and putting words into the participants' mouths.

"The video editor kept looking at me, and after each of my unsolicited answers to my own question, he'd give a thumbs-down and say, 'Hmm, think we better cut that.' After all the edits, we wound up with a pretty good video on what the sessions should look like, but it in no way resembled the actual discovery and action dialogue we had just filmed! It was a humbling experience, but even a simple 'reformed MRSA transmitter' like me was able to learn from it!"

As a result of Dr. Lloyd's epiphany (which, not surprisingly, was appreciated by most of his "always in control" colleagues at the other beta site hospitals), the "twenty-second-deep-breath-and-be-silent" PD mantra evolved. Twenty seconds is an eternity (long enough to sing all of "Happy Birthday") when you know the answer and are waiting for it to emerge from a group of silent others.

The "twenty-second rule" has become standard operating procedure for facilitators at all PD MRSA events. During the facilitators' self-imposed twenty seconds of silence, a participant at a DAD, unit briefing, or PD core team meeting invariably fills the silence. Nature abhors a vacuum—but apparently not half as much as health care providers.

FIVE

Early Wins, Squandered Gains

Pioneering the PD Process at Merck

*Pharmaceutical manufacturer Merck provided the first
full-fledged opportunity to apply the positive deviance
process in a company. One of the most successful pharmaceutical companies in the world, Merck products are sold
in more than 140 countries and the company employs a
worldwide workforce of nearly sixty thousand people. The
firm is an oft-cited exemplar of a well-managed global enterprise.[1] Richard traces the achievements of the pilot effort in
Mexico and its surprising aftermath.*

IN THE SUMMER OF 2005, MERCK, long a darling of Wall
Street, was feeling the heat. Its decades-long track record of
introducing new blockbuster drugs had hit a five-year dry spell. One product, Vioxx, highly significant to its earnings stream, had been voluntarily
withdrawn after publicity on possible side effects and FDA scrutiny.[2]

Merck was under enormous pressure to deliver earnings. A high stock
price to corporate earnings ratio was essential to acquire promising companies with stock and use their patents to fill its shrinking pipeline. These
strategic calculations were felt through the ranks. Only a handful of
drugs still retained patent protection (thereby commanding high profits).

Several would soon come off patent and compete with generic alternatives. High priority was assigned to grow market share to compensate for shrinking margins.

Merck Mexico had a particular problem. Poor performance of the osteoporosis "miracle drug," Fosamax, stood out like ink stains on a white dress shirt. Mexico ranked last among all countries in which the product was sold, and management seemed incapable of correcting this performance shortfall. Headquarters called constantly. Tensions rose. Jobs were on the line.

Readers, having been exposed to a litany of intractable societal ills—from FGM eradication to malnutrition—might easily dismiss the "Fosamax problem" as an insignificant corporate hiccup. All is in the eye of the beholder. Shifting Mexico's worst-in-class Fosamax standing had been as resistant to improvement as reducing MRSA infections in hospitals. Careers depended on it.

A far more radical challenge lurked unseen. Precisely because the problem could not be solved through business as usual, Merck Mexico would have to tackle its cultural orthodoxies and constitutional framework of top-down, command-and-control solutions. Let there be no doubt, this undertaking incurred political risk for those leading the charge. The corporate immune defense response would mobilize itself to repel the invaders at the beachhead.

Some at headquarters were casting about for outside-the-box answers. An article on positive deviance in *Fast Company* magazine caught the attention of Grey Warner, vice president of Merck's pharma business in Latin America. His territory extended from Mexico to Tierra del Fuego. Warner had concluded that the pharma industry's traditional business model was broken and needed to be reinvented. With blockbuster drugs coming off patent and generics cannibalizing revenue streams, new product introductions could no longer be counted upon. A breakthrough in sales and marketing might offer a way outside the box. Could Merck pull off a disruptive change in its relationships with hospitals and doctors and gain market share? Could the company move from being just a typical provider of pharmaceuticals to a trusted member of the health care club? In the sweltering summer of 2005, Warner posed this challenge to his extended management team and offered the idea of positive deviance as a possible way forward.

We have previously noted that an invitation is essential to the integrity of the PD process. Warner made it clear to those assembled that they could opt in or opt out. Most of those present abstained. Tentatively, the director of sales and marketing for Mexico, Andres Bruzual, expressed interest. His predicament was a layup for PD. Bruzual had exhausted every trick in Merck's repertoire to address the Fosamax sales problem. PD beckoned as an alternative of last resort.

In February 2005 he broached the idea of pilot testing PD at the quarterly district manager meeting in Mexico City. The austere corporate meeting room was arranged in a classroom-style configuration. Bruzual, a six-foot-tall Venezuelan with a crew cut, is charismatic and tightly wired. A take-charge kind of guy, he fills the room with energy. His kickoff was distinctly out of character: "This will be driven by your passion, not by me," he said. Quizzical exchange of glances. There was no precedent whatsoever for Bruzual deferring to the whims of subordinates or being guided by their "passion." None could recall being invited to take the ball and run with it, and most couldn't believe it would happen. Many were skeptical as to how this would play out. Of forty-one district managers overseeing a field sales force of over 224 local sales reps in Mexico, half volunteered to stick around and learn what PD was all about.

An orientation was held the next day, introducing the concept and its successes in the developing world. Then Bruzual concluded with an unprecedented invitation: "So there it is," he said. "I leave it up to you to decide whether or not you want to try the PD idea and what to try it on if you choose to do so."

"It is almost impossible to overstate the extent to which this isn't Merck," states David Raimondo, chief of staff for the region. "It's a glass-half-empty place. In the face of poor sales, the conventional solution is to target something as 'broken' and impose a top-down get-well program." Raimondo continues: "You couldn't find a more unlikely personality to sponsor a process like this. Andres is central casting's iconic manager—General Patton with a Spanish accent. His persona elicits commitment and followership. But he relented to PD's cornerstone principles of a bottom-up process."

That's because Bruzual was desperate. Having taken a leap of faith, he played by the rules. He was fastidious in waiting out the long, pregnant silence that followed after his offer. Finally someone spoke. Eventually the participants came up with their own topic and how they would organize to tackle it.

Unsurprisingly, the focus of the PD initiative would be Fosamax, which, as previously noted, had proven unresponsive to a sequence of campaigns to spur sales and market share. Notwithstanding global volume of $3.2 billion, the half-life of the product was ebbing away. Its patent was expiring in 2008. Fosamax was one of the few blockbusters in Merck's offering where proven product superiority guaranteed high margins—if the company could just sell more of it. Bruzual needed to seize the moment before the window of opportunity was closed by generic alternatives.

It is relevant to grasp that Merck is a highly systematized, results-oriented place. The firm has metrics for everything. One is a "product evolution index." A score of 100 means a product is growing as fast as the market. Fosamax Mexico was scoring in the seventies—in other words, losing ground to competition. Of forty-one districts (each district consisting of a half dozen reps and one district manager), only six were meeting quota and maintaining market share. From a PD perspective, these positive exceptions were observable fact. With similar marketing budgets, sales coverage, and demographics, they were outperforming the pack.

This discrepancy was the hook that mobilized the district managers (DMs) to test the PD concept.

"PD certainly unleashed a novel approach," confirms Bruzual. "For the first time, I was looking for answers from the grass roots instead of giving them an answer. But it was slow and painful. Only half of the district managers came back the second day, and most of those seemed reluctant to take the reins. I reflected on why. We're products of classic conditioning. Over two decades here, truth is most solutions come from the top. We had to approach things differently if we expected to discover different answers. But I was upending the culture of the place."

Inertia and the Prevailing Psychological Contract

Time for the pause button. Bruzual's narrative calls attention to the district managers' hesitation to buy into a process that might give them greater voice and control of their destiny. Why? Companies foster an implicit employment contract in which employee contributions and deference to authority are traded in exchange for compensation, a career path, and some measure of job security. In effect, we trade personal discretion, freedom, and latitude for independent action as the price of membership in a company. As witnessed by the reluctance of DMs to take initiative, this "contract" is deeply embedded. And it takes considerable effort to alter it—not just by executives but by employees as well. That's why an authentic bottom-up process (such as the positive deviance approach) is not an easy sell. Employees are conditioned to go with the flow and follow directions. Accordingly, they need to witness a great deal of management conviction (and behavior consistent with words) to overcome disbelief and fear of retribution for breaking the old contract for a yet-to-be-proven new one.

Bottom-up change is far easier if the authority structure allows leadership to be exercised from the ranks below. One witnesses this at high-performing retailers such as Nordstrom and in the transplants of

Japanese automotive manufacturers such as Honda in Marysville, Ohio, or Toyota's Nummi facility in Fremont, California. But it is a rare condition in most Western firms and a blatantly heretical one at Merck.

There is also political risk for leaders such as Bruzual who elect to experiment in the "participative" domain. Countercultural happenings are hard to hide. They generate disequilibrium that reverberates far from the epicenter. Word gets around: "Andres is doing something weird in Mexico!" It is essential to protect such guerrilla leaders who pick up the baton. Those in authority—in this case, Grey Warner (Bruzual's boss) and Bruzual himself—need to provide air cover, insulate the initiative from the skeptics, and pass the no-bullshit test from dubious subordinates that their commitment is authentic. Management must resist the impulse to take charge. They must legitimize the challenge as important and be convincing that they can't solve it themselves. This, by the way, is often experienced by managers as a tacit confession of inadequacy (given implicit expectations that "you're the boss and get paid a lot for having the answers"). A bottom-up process is an unnatural act within a traditional hierarchy. It disturbs equilibrium. And payoff is far from guaranteed.

Tentative Beginnings

Following the workshop, a core team of five district managers met to discuss next steps. One remembers: "We sat there looking at each other. What had we gotten ourselves into? Yes, we had an idea of how PD worked, but would it work here? Skepticism arose from Merck's long history of management gimmicks. Was this the flavor of the month?"

Belief systems foreclose the possibility of change. A defining encounter with this obstacle arose in Mali when tackling the high incidence of malnutrition and illness among children (see "The Sorcerer?").

"We rolled up our sleeves," recalls one team member. "Timing-wise, we were at a critical juncture. Mexico had a chance to redeem itself.

The Sorcerer?

Merck and Mali would seem to have little in common. Except "sorcerers." In sub-Saharan Mali, prevailing beliefs attributed the widespread affliction of childhood disease and infant mortality to the village witch. The will of the "sorcerer" was immutable, and villagers unquestioningly accepted this as a fact of life. Nothing could prevail against the sorcerer's spells. Change seemed impossible.

Representatives from Save the Children working to address widespread malnutrition engaged the community in the positive deviance process. As in Vietnam, the jumping-off point for the process was the somersault question: "Are there any families with well-nourished children?" Villagers acknowledged that a few children in the community were, in fact, rarely sick or lethargic. Through the process that followed, the community discovered that the parents of the healthy children engaged in behaviors that were different from those of the parents of the sick children. Whereas the majority had never conceived of food as medicine, PD families recognized the connection. Children were given additional midday snacks, and everyone in the home washed their hands with soap and water. Fathers of healthy children were also more actively involved in mealtimes and helped decide whether their youngsters needed to go to the clinic, normally a decision that was the sole prerogative of grandfathers.

As the parents of the malnourished children began emulating their neighbors' counterconventional behaviors, their own children grew healthier, too. Reassessing child health status a half year later cemented a communitywide epiphany: malnutrition was no longer an affliction beyond their control. They didn't achieve this through an understanding of calories or vitamins or bacterial contaminants. Rather, they internalized the change through their own experience and culture. A wizened grandmother summed the shared sense of triumph with the proclamation: "On a vaincu les sorcerers!" (We have vanquished the sorcerers!)

Field conditions in Mali have parallels in the corporate world. We can imagine the corridor conversations at Merck Mexico that assigned the blame for Fosamax's poor performance—along with the responsibility for fixing it—to those in authority. Superstitions such as "Headquarters makes us do unproductive things" or "Don't bother; the boss already has the answer" create Dilbert-like vestiges of Mali's villagers, resigned to the corporate sorcerer. The turning point in Mexico City arrived when the blame game and self-imposed impotence gave way to learning about what was working on the front lines.

PD appealed because it focuses on our best performers. Strange idea: celebrate *them* rather than condemning those who are not doing as well. The magic of PD is that it isn't best practice (where superiors bludgeon everyone into doing something based on somebody else's success somewhere else). PD appealed because we could figure it out for ourselves."

"Putting us in charge forestalled our usual passive resistance," states Hector Ruiz, another member of the group. "When we're subjected to top-down edicts, we routinely ask for relief, negotiating with Bruzual to offload other work. But in this case *we* owned the initiative, and had no leverage to ask for offsets in exchange for the extra workload. As it was up to us to decide who would do what, we absorbed the extra workload into our budgets and calendars."

A plan and a timeline were established. Then the timetable began to slip. Skepticism blossomed at headquarters like algae in a stagnant fishpond: "The district managers aren't interested" was the corridor conversation. But Bruzual held steady. "Be patient," he said, "they just have conflicting priorities." By May, one team had conducted its focus groups. "This lit a fire under the others," states district manager Takeshi Nakauma. "When we wrapped up phase one, we had reached three-quarters of the 224 sales reps in the country. Data provided a solid baseline of common practices. We began to hear recurring mentions of reps who might be potential PDs."

A month later, two hundred sales reps from around the country gathered in Mexico City. A mixture of anticipation and skepticism filled the repurposed hotel ballroom. Following a very brief description of the concept of positive deviance and its application in Vietnam, tables of coded data for Fosamax sales were distributed with sales rep names and district numbers blanked out. "Data showed the good, the bad, and the ugly," recalls one of the DMs present. "No one knew which rep was which. It soon became evident to the reps that the district managers had no predetermined answers. In self-organized groups of eight, the sales reps were asked to identify the high-performing districts and contemplate practices that correlated with better results. Salient findings were written on Post-its and organized into clusters."

Merck was engaged in a process that tapped the ingenuity and practical field knowledge of its people (i.e., the individual nodes of intelligence). This kind of engagement takes hold when a quest is sufficiently aspirational or urgent that people come to believe their participation is critical to success. Once engagement kicks in, the social system (heretofore frozen into patterns appropriate for business as usual) can, through the PD process, harness energy and challenge orthodoxies. In effect, the group looks in the mirror, decides what makes sense, and determines what to do about it.

Meaningful change must bridge between intellectual awareness "that change is needed" on one hand and the new behavior that makes change real on the other. The second part, as previously noted, requires changes in the social context. Without realizing it, Bruzual was reconfiguring the social system by letting the DMs take the lead. They, in turn, gave the work over to the sales reps. It became apparent: "Management has no answers up their sleeve. It's up to us!" The reps began to believe that their help was really necessary to interpret the data.

With the sales reps now in the loop, it was time for a second round of field conversations. This time the district managers targeted potential PDs. Pairs of district managers traveled to each city. Their mission was to zoom in on unusual practices.

Takeshi Nakauma from the core group recalls: "Interviewing the PD reps was like following a trail of breadcrumbs. Whereas the average sales- man was adhering to standards (i.e., management's sales productivity checklist), exceptional people were throwing the rulebook away. Amazing. They were improvising to stay in synch with the doctors and deepening those relationships."

A back story is warranted here. Merck's sales management embraced a set of orthodoxies venerated as the "Ten Commandments" in running its geographically dispersed sales force. Two, in particular, were tracked obsessively: (1) sales volume by drug category (as *the* indicator of sales rep performance), and (2) the "Rule of Seven" (i.e., reps must make seven sales calls per day to meet the company's productivity standards). District managers were the enforcers of this code. (That's why they—not sales reps—were made the centerpiece of the PD process and did the inter- views. Andres Bruzual was convinced that the *district managers*, more than the reps themselves, needed to change mind-set and behavior.) Interviews were confirming that scattered across Mexico were a few standout sales reps with novel shortcuts to productivity, imaginative ways of positioning products, and personal touches that made them a trusted partner with the doctors.

People in organizations make thousands of decisions, and these sum to define an organization's trajectory. The arc of these internalized "truths" is invisible but inexorable: How "big" does an opportunity have to be to be "interesting"? How are budgets negotiated? How is analysis translated into financial projections and how do projections in turn pre-configure the aperture of the possible? What are the consequences for missing financial targets? For making mistakes? These interpretations reinforce the conventional wisdom about "the way things work around here."[3] When adaptive change becomes necessary, subtle undercurrents embedded in the social system can inflict death by a thousand cuts and undermine needed change. Companies—particularly successful and well-established ones—are often ensnared in a belief system that worked brilliantly in the past but becomes incongruent with new realities.

Core team member Fa Leo adds: "Initially, the reps felt that our interviews were aimed at 'getting dirt on their boss.' Participation in Mexico City began to change that. They could see our focus was on field outcomes, not supervisory behavior. They began to speak up. 'Hey, this is a chance to tell it like it is.' We began to hear about behavior at variance to the rules. They told us what they were *really* doing versus what their managers thought they were doing. We realized how little the district managers knew. Example: reps are supposed to use a handheld computer to track sales and profile customers—a Merck standard. But they said things like, 'We don't use them. It's just a reporting device to headquarters.' Or, 'Time spent entering data into handhelds takes time from working with doctors.' Scales were falling from our eyes."

Somewhere in this second round, many district managers had an epiphany. Some reps were exhibiting extraordinary ingenuity and achieving extraordinary results. That's when many became believers. They were discovering useful tricks of the trade that had been invisible. A district manager expressed his surprise: "Very interesting stuff. At first I was shocked. 'Handhelds not important!' That's heresy! 'Marketing material is irrelevant'—wow! But as it sank in, I was getting insight into the counterproductive side effects of our productivity measures."

Having interviewed fifteen possible PDs, district managers narrowed the list to twelve whose approaches seemed most replicable. But instead of declaring these "best practices," they reconvened all sales reps for a second time. The venue was the ballroom of the Royal Hotel, Mexico City. More than two hundred attended, arranging themselves in small groups. There were no tables. Each group had a flip chart. Findings of common and uncommon behaviors were debated. Throughout the day the DMs emphasized: "This stuff belongs to you. The practices belong to you."

The biggest surprise to many—both sales reps and district managers alike—was that the "Rule of Seven" was getting in the way. PDs making three calls per day were routinely outperforming those who made seven. The rule was actually hurting Fosamax results.

Some subgroups had a PD in their circle, but neither they nor the PD knew it. When discussion turned to one of the uncommon practices, the unknowing PD might say, "Well, I do that. I give presents to the doctor. Isn't that normal?" The rest would reply, "No, not at all." Another was doing a great job with client education. Instead of just sending out obligatory invitations to doctors for Merck-sponsored lectures, this individual called doctors before the agenda was set, solicited ideas for topics, enrolled them in the event's design, and invited them to participate on a panel. A big "wow" for many. The key to success in the relationship with the doctor is ingenious "little things"—sending birthday cards, attending a doctor's son's graduation, bringing a favorite food from another territory. Reps were learning from each other. There was a lot of give and take. District managers observed from the sidelines and did not intrude on group discussions.

The session was designed to conclude with time for all reps to write up their takeaways for their return to the field on Monday. It was pouring rain, and given rush-hour traffic in Mexico City (ugly on the best of days), the sponsors decided to adjourn the session so people could go home at 3 p.m. Yet most stayed until 5:30 and completed their personal action plans. The meeting ended with two hundred individuals committing to an uncommon behavior that was appropriate to their situation.

Results? Extraordinary! By the end of the year in which the project was launched, all districts met quota. One year later, the same population of sales reps was 30 percent above quota, an exceptional achievement. District managers witnessed veterans adopting the PD behaviors voluntarily, not out of obligation or compliance. Many formerly "exceptional" behaviors have since become commonplace. (One of the attributes of the PD approach is that the exceptional behaviors stick.) The "Rule of Seven" is now only a guideline. A number of the PDs have been promoted, a by-product of their results and visibility through the process. Of the twenty-five district managers who participated extensively, most report a change in their outlook and management philosophy.

Early Wins, Squandered Gains

Given the impressive results, readers may be startled to learn that Merck's successful application of PD remained confined to the Fosamax sales force in Mexico. Why? As Bruzual notes, sponsorship requires executives who are truly willing to empower those in the ranks below them and hold steady during the time it takes to discover things. Mustering commitment isn't just a matter of waking up one morning and deciding to give positive deviance a try. It requires political will to engage in adaptive work. "For one brief moment," states Fa Leo, "Andres had all the ducks in line: Grey Warner was an advocate, as was his team at corporate. All bought in. But counterparts elsewhere in other businesses responsible for other pharmaceutical lines or geographies didn't buy the idea."

"We cannot say the big uptick in Fosamax sales that followed was 100 percent the result of PD," observes Bruzual. "We had simultaneously released Fosamax Plus—an improved formulation. This muddies the metrics a little. Still, the PDs continued to do better than the pack, even with

Fosamax Plus. In any case, our pre-PD baseline was 39 percent market share. Post PD, we had 45 percent market share—highest in the world." Today, Mexico's Fosamax share still ranks near the top.

Political Capital and Organizational Drift

The gains were significant—but so were the costs. "This kind of process needs a lot of noise, news, attention, buzz, and enthusiasm," reflects Bruzual. "If the senior sponsors aren't deeply committed, you can't sustain something like this. Most organizations have a big, powerful constituency for 'what is' but almost no constituency for 'what could be.'

"It's very energy intensive," he continues. "It took some doing to convince my immediate boss to get a hotel for the district managers and to pay travel costs for reps to attend the session. We had to justify hijacking teams from their day jobs on the street. Mexico is a huge country. Travel time and travel costs add up. Consider the scale—forty-one district managers and over two hundred sales reps. All this took eight months. We had to piggyback off routine cycle meetings to reach people and disseminate what we were learning. If my general manager hadn't bought in, it wouldn't have happened.

"When you try to do something like this," Bruzual concludes, "you draw on precious resources: money—and especially time. Taking sales reps out of the field for a day means they're not calling on doctors. People get nervous. Merck (and the pharma industry as a whole) is a very old-style, traditional business. We've been doing things one way for one hundred fifty years. Until recently, Merck has been very successful. You become arrogant. There is little latitude for self-examination—and little openness to change."

There is a term for the undertow that draws organizations toward traditional patterns. It is called "organizational drift," and it exercises influence subliminally. Existing political arrangements usually ensure that novel initiatives rarely get a fair day in court. The weapon of choice for protecting the status quo is the "precaucus" veto (a stealth device for sidelining bold new ideas), often framed in economic terms. As the value of money spent is more quantifiable than the value of opportunities lost (e.g., the opportunity cost of taking a salesman away from the field for a day is more measurable, at least in the short term, than any potential gain), the burden of proof lies with the initiators of change. Unsurprisingly, the status quo prevails. Remember that those on top have made it in the current system, and they see little personal value in changing what they know and can succeed in—especially when challenged by ideas like positive deviance that are detached from the orthodoxies that undergird their historical success.

People in authority do not generally see themselves as simply defending the status quo or avoiding the risks of change. At Merck they saw themselves as protecting the operating system and cultural norms upon which a large, global enterprise was built. Destabilizing this essential discipline is not taken lightly. The challenge, of course, in companies as in nature, is to foster sufficient adaptation to the changing environment to remain competitive while at the same time conserving those qualities that remain relevant.

Perspective on differing contexts for the exercise and alignment of authority is warranted here. In Vietnam, Egypt, and the Pittsburgh VA hospital, more attention was given to achieving alignment—or at minimum acquiescence—from those in charge. And in most of the examples in this book, authority was diffused. Village-level buy-in was sufficient to get a PD process up and running. Ministerial authority in Hanoi, Cairo, Kampala, or Islamabad was unlikely to stand in the way of success once efficacy was proven. In hospitals, alarming MRSA transmission rates were actually killing patients—a burning platform that few could ignore. At Merck, by way of contrast, Grey Warner did not attempt to enroll the broader authority structure above him or even to syndicate this initiative with functional and geographic peers at his level. Within his own span of control, only one of his subordinates, Bruzual, volunteered to try PD. Others opted out. Further, no effort was made to evangelize any of these stakeholders as the initiative gained momentum. Add to the mix Merck's command-and-control tradition, far more pervasive and rigorous than generally encountered in villages, countries, and even hospitals, and the lack of uptake becomes more understandable.

Barriers to the Diffusion of Innovation

Though Bruzual was instrumental in the success achieved in Mexico, it is noteworthy that when rotated into a new assignment in Chile, he didn't repeat his initiative there. Why? "Support from my Chilean country manager wasn't in place," he explains. "And my successor in Mexico was, let's say, 'a different kind of manager.' He let the approach languish, notwithstanding the Fosamax beachhead. My district managers in Mexico have been hesitant to apply it elsewhere as well."

When pressed, Bruzual elaborated on why PD hadn't diffused beyond Fosamax and Mexico. "'Not invented here' is always latent in an organization's immune defense system," he states. "Even after we got a great write-up in the *London Times* (which we disseminated), people said: 'Yes, but that's Mexico. We're not Mexico; we're different.' The general manager of Argentina read the report on our results. 'Is this really true?' he asked, betraying his skepticism. We sent him audited documentation of results. No response. Nothing crystallized in other countries. A few tried but failed for lack of sponsorship."

David Gasser, a senior staff member of Bruzual's executive team, elaborates on the dilutive effect of incessant job rotations. "You crush the momentum of a process like this when you change senior leadership and transfer the champions. Success was a brilliant but fragile flower in the Merck jungle. It needed prolonged nurturance. Job rotations break up the symbiotic networks you've created. The fragile ecology that fostered change never reaches the critical mass necessary to become self-perpetuating." Gasser makes an important point here. Prior to PD, successes had occurred in intact communities (including hospitals) where the stakeholder group was relatively stable. The argument for job rotation in big companies, of course, is that it cross-trains talent and helps break down functional silos by introducing different perspectives. All true. But it is absolutely toxic to efforts aimed at building a critical mass of Jesuits dedicated to the new gospel. Constant churn ensures that the advocacy of individual converts will be trumped by institutional memory.

Lessons Learned

"What did I learn personally?" Bruzual asks rhetorically. "In this industry you are told what to do. By the time you get to my level, it is an unnatural act to free up people to do what *they* think they need to do. PD has had an impact on my leadership approach. I have gone from being directive to being more empowering. It was a personal learning experience."

Bruzual's subordinates noted a change in his style. (They initially worried Bruzual was ill, as he was so atypically nondirective.) "Today he listens more and asks more questions," states Raimondo. "He has learned how to mobilize the troops. Vestiges of the experience are embedded in his behavior. But he is a tiny minority in this huge enterprise; indeed he was unique among his peers in Mexico."

The man who started the whole thing, Grey Warner, reflects on results both bitter and sweet. "I've probably done more with many of these tools than anyone else. But overall, not a lot has happened since. I'm certain that the people involved speak to each other in a different way (peer to peer, peer to boss). They approach work in a different way. At the finale in Mexico City we went around the room asking people for their impressions. One rep, not a PD himself, said, 'I've seen how small things can make a big difference.' PD has manifested itself in the way individuals are more involved and in the way they go about working."

Reflections

The sustained turnaround of Fosamax sales at Merck confirms that the PD process can work in companies. But the aftermath raises intriguing questions. Why the lack of diffusion elsewhere? Is there an inverse correlation between tightly managed companies like Merck and PD's prospects? Is there something about corporate management that confines successes to isolated beachheads?

Merck epitomizes the classic standard model: socially engineered, top-down, authority driven. As mentioned briefly in chapter 1, this worldview holds that uncertainty and risk can be mitigated by meticulous planning, direction, and control. This framework promises greater predictability and reduces executive performance anxiety. Authors, consultants, and management gurus have invested decades railing against the limitations of this approach with little headway. Peel the onion, and we discover a root system entwined around orthodoxies that hold it fast in our repertoire. Not least among these, as noted earlier in this chapter, is the psychological contract that undergirds employee service to an enterprise.

The standard model has a lot going for it. It *seems* to be the most efficient way of getting from here to there. For technical problems involving "known knowns" (e.g., launching a marketing campaign) or "known unknowns" (e.g., the protocols for human trials for a promising new compound), it is exactly the right approach to take.

Alfred North Whitehead once said: "Civilization advances by extending the number of operations which we can perform without thinking about them."[4] One of the many virtues of the standard model is just this: the more that can be accomplished through productive routines, the less potential waste from improvisation and reinventing the wheel.

Bruzual's comments underscore that Merck, like most corporations, has a well-honed set of such protocols that meet the frugality test. When a choice arises between relying on a proven top-down approach (albeit even in situations where it may be stretched to the limits of applicability) versus an iffy, amorphous, hard-to-predict, bottom-up process, the familiar seems the better bet. It takes less time. Why abandon the proven in favor of the problematic?

On the whole, companies are remarkably efficient organisms. (And the market makes quick work of underperformers.) Sophisticated tools used in a modern enterprise give management reasonable basis for confidence that decisions from above translate into proximate action. Real-time information, financial controls, and operating tools (like Six Sigma, business process engineering, pay for performance, and other incentives) are, all in all, efficient and effective.

Like many companies, Merck operates under assumptions of scarcity. Almost universally, scarce resources are allocated via central authority. It is an effective way to make trade-offs, resolve conflicts over competing priorities, and lower transaction costs. Recall that Bruzual was sensitive to his use of investment dollars, head count, and sales force time. Scarcity is built into Merck's genetic code. Start with this premise and many of the inhibitions against experimenting with an approach like PD become self evident. Scarcity, not abundance, is as foundational to management hierarchy as royal bloodlines have been to monarchies since Babylon. It preserves the order of things.

Mitigating Risk and Avoiding Failure

Corporations are averse to failure. And to their credit, its occurrence is episodic—an outlier condition. When failure occurs, causes are analyzed and preventive measures implemented. (See "The Spectrum of Process Standardization.") Relying on contemporary management tools and

The Spectrum of Process Standardization

Process standardization works best when inputs are relatively consistent and an operating model can be built to deal with contingencies and produce reliable results. As we saw at Merck, standardization gets more difficult when nuances matter more than commonalities, and when cause and effect relationships are unclear.

Consider a continuum with corporations at one end and civil society, informal communities, villages, and refugee camps on the other. NGOs, government organizations, schools, and hospitals are probably somewhere in between. Placement on the scale is determined not so much by structure or hierarchy (indeed, hospitals and many communities in the developing world rank high in both) but by the confidence that those in authority have in the correlation between cause and effect.

The modern corporation anchors one end of the continuum because of its emphasis on strategic intent and the considerable energy invested to hardwire these intentions and drive corresponding actions and desired results. (Mechanisms for doing so include organizational structure, transfer pricing, key performance indicators, pay for performance, and so forth.) Within a wide range of normal circumstances (earlier referred to as "technical" challenges), top-down exercise of these technical tools by leaders in companies is sufficient to adequately assess perturbations in the environment and execute appropriate course corrections. Less buttoned-down organizations—universities, schools, communities, and hospitals (with highly independent and less-aligned stakeholder groups) or NGOs (where member loyalty and alignment is often motivated by service to higher-order values)—are generally not as responsive. By corporate standards, "no one is really in charge."

processes, employees can be depended upon to execute a corrective plan. Executives have reasonable confidence that if they declare "rudder hard right" the ship will turn to starboard. One triumph of modern management is this legacy of tightly coupled operating systems that usually work.

Consider this: maybe failure is less the exception in noncorporate settings. (Some might argue it is more the norm.) Corporations work on the premise that they can weed out infrequent failure via rational analysis and the disciplined application of management science. More loosely coupled organizations (e.g., villages, NGOs, universities, etc.) experience these corporate management tools as problematic. Positive deviance (focusing on those who succeed against all odds) is appealing when one is not as certain the organization can march directly from A to B. The PD process starts with what is succeeding and works backward.

Limitations of the Standard Model

Einstein once said: "Everything should be made as simple as possible—but not simpler." And there's the rub. Yes, there *are* many good reasons to rely on the standard model most of the time. But, true to Einstein's cautionary quote, simple remedies can at times be simplistic. There are circumstances where the standard model doesn't work. Trouble is, it is hard to spot these cases *ex ante*.

A bottom-up process interjects diversity. This enlarges what we call "the solution space." Up to a point more diversity means more adaptive capacity. Small and obscure components—easily overlooked—can be vital (we witnessed this at Genentech and Merck). Attention to detail matters, and attention to small details matters a lot.[5] In nature, such detail is manifested in gene pools and tiny mutations. Organizational mutations occur among those closest to the action via small adaptations in the face of adversity or opportunity. Those closer to the bottom of the organizational pyramid (for example, in companies where delivery of services or the manufacture of products actually takes place) participate in "experiments" every day. But the standard model isn't especially well geared to listening, let alone learning through this bottom-up channel. As described earlier, Merck Mexico discovered, as part of a positive deviance inquiry, that a few aberrant sales reps had experimented, learned, and established innovative pathways to success. They had made microadaptations to the microclimate of Mexico—notwithstanding Merck's systemic guidelines for its global sales force. The missed opportunity, of course, was that Merck needed myriad microadaptations of this kind to optimize in each microclimate and compete. But high-decibel directives of the standard model drowned out quiet discoveries from below. Unsurprisingly, these remained invisible to management until the PD process brought them to light.

The biggest limitation of the standard model is that it takes process standardization too far. It loses its potency when local knowledge and aesthetic judgment matter. Adaptive work is judgment intensive and craft dependent. Variability between one situation and the next matters. One-size-fits-all protocols fail. Grey Warner's ambition to reinvent Merck's relationships with the doctors grasped the importance of all this in his quest to differentiate Merck from competition.

The case for tapping the distributed intelligence of the community that needs to change is not advocated as an end in itself or inspired by an ideology of "empowerment," "employee participation," or "workplace democracy." The success in Mexico demonstrates that the rank and file need to be engaged because they often discover ingenious ways to deliver better results. It is also the best way not only of capturing what they know but of enabling them to change what they do.

Can PD Work in Companies?

These reflections highlight many factors in for-profit enterprises that make adaptation of the positive deviance approach difficult. But it is not impossible. The next section describes a highly successful adaptation of PD at Goldman Sachs. It offers a provocative contrast to Merck because both firms were: 1) trying to understand what made some salesmen more productive, and 2) spread successes cultivated in one region to other geographically dispersed units. Sales forces are ideal for testing assumptions about performance and change. Salespeople typically exercise more latitude for independent action day to day than their counterparts on assembly lines or in office cubicles. Owing to the propensity toward greater variation in performance, commission-based incentives are employed to align corporate and individual goals. All this extra leeway creates fertile ground for positive deviants. We observed this at Merck. Goldman Sachs provides a more encouraging counterpoint, engaging its wealth advisors in identifying the PDs in their midst, learning what they were up to, and giving individuals the freedom to opt in or opt out of applying lessons learned. Few declined the invitation. Within two years, these ideas had spread across all eleven regions in the United States.

Leveraging the Positive Deviants at Goldman Sachs

Goldman Sachs's Private Wealth Management unit had experienced a string of controversial top-down change initiatives.[6] On one hand, the field force of three hundred investment advisors felt railroaded by New York's radical policy shifts and top-down edicts. On the other, headquarters felt thwarted in achieving the pace of change needed to stay in step with the marketplace.

Investment professionals (IPs) in the field historically operated independently or as two- or three-person teams. Each unit evolved highly idiosyncratic approaches to the work of persuading high-net-worth individuals to entrust the teams with the management of their money. Success in this work depended on performance, of course, but also on building deep, trusting relationships with wealthy clients that often lasted for decades. These clients invited their IPs to weddings, bar mitzvahs, and graduation ceremonies that extended relationships to their heirs. For this reason, IPs remained notoriously independent of the company itself. When they moved to another firm, their clients would typically follow. To an uncommon degree, power favored the field force—not the traditional corporate hierarchy.

On the other side of this classic field-versus-headquarters schism was Goldman Sachs's top management, deeply concerned that the industry was undergoing a transformation of disruptive proportions. Investment firms were under pressure to deliver greater transparency and compliance oversight while simultaneously reducing their brokerage fees. How could Goldman Sachs retain its existing wealthy clients, improve its profitability, and grow its assets in a turbulent and increasingly competitive environment? Management's solution? Transform the IPs' approach from a process that relied heavily on brokerage income to one focused on fee-based advice. But the IPs resisted the policy shift—and this was maddening to their seniors. The business case for change was compelling—it was all there in PowerPoint. Why didn't the field force's knowledge of the SWOT analysis translate into an appetite to actually change what they were doing? Management tweaked and rejiggered their pitch—a simple application of knowledge management. The assumption was: if we just get the right communication formula, we can inoculate the many disbelievers.

David Dechman, cohead of the U.S. Private Wealth Management (PWM) unit, found himself at the epicenter of the impasse. By late 2001, the PWM unit was feeling the full impact of the gridlock of the stakeholders. Dechman's chosen path was to relinquish his role as an authority figure and to let go of top management's deep attachment to "better knowledge management" or "more directives" as the solution. He exercised leadership by asking the individual IPs one arresting question: "Are some teams, with similar territories and prospects, able to thrive in this difficult climate?" In short, Dechman engaged the reps in tapping their own wisdom.

David Dechman had never heard of the positive deviance process. But the stubbornness of the problem he faced and the independence of those he sought to mobilize drew him intuitively to design a process that was identical in every important respect.

A six-person council of influential IPs spearheaded a "sales force effectiveness" inquiry. The council's task was to catalog common practices and subsequently identify exceptionally successful approaches. Its members assured the rank and file that any findings would be subjected to the acid test of relevance and scalability (e.g., what was working for the best team in Boston would have to be transferable to Dallas).

Phase one invested two months in focus groups involving IPs across the system. Interviews of peers established a baseline of common practices and occasionally surfaced an unusual angle that seemed to be working. Phase two focused on discovery, talking in depth to potential PDs. Phase three coalesced these findings. Teams (composed in part of individuals already using the practices as well as those who had become advocates along the way) carried the momentum forward. Five practices seemed especially relevant. The teams were then charged with coming up with an action learning design such that every team in the country could be exposed to the ideas, debate them, and implement them on a voluntary basis.

When it was time to disseminate, teams that had identified the PD practices became the pointy end of the spear. They visited each office and described why and how their particular practice worked. There was one person on each team from each office, so one of the presenting IPs could double as a local resource on the topic. When local teams had questions later, they could turn to their resource person. The approach generated an amazing buzz—primarily because each team could witness what others "just like me" were doing that was yielding better results.

Phase three of the process involved building a system to measure progress toward goals and to track trends over time. Dechman ranked each of the eleven regional offices on their incorporation of the five practices, and he publicized results. The process relied exclusively on transparency and peer review. No sanctions for nonadoption were imposed. People automatically felt good about being on top or bad about being on the bottom. This sustained attention when backsliding might have otherwise set in.

Goldman Sachs management had tried and failed to communicate the threatening market changes using analysis-based, classroom-like briefings. Sometimes this technique works. But explicit knowledge, conventionally delivered like pizza (neat boxes with toppings of concepts, theories, best practices, and war stories), is consumed by the brain but not metabolized into action. The learning we call intuition, know-how, and common sense gets into the bloodstream through osmosis. It is shaped by social context. Management needed to tackle this to progress.

During the course of this endeavor, old rivalries between formerly competing teams of investment professionals subsided. For the first time in memory, a sense of "we win together" emerged as the new ethic. Skepticism gave way to conviction as the wealth advisors overcame their own exceptionalism. The PD approach, implemented over eighteen months, profoundly altered behavior, practice, and performance. The business unit got a jump on the competition. Three years later, the Private Wealth Management unit had doubled in size and was singled out by the firm and its shareholders as the business it wanted to grow most aggressively. Average productivity per wealth advisor nearly doubled, team size has increased, and the fee-based business model has achieved near-universal acceptance.

Results

The case study at Merck and the contrasting example at Goldman Sachs describe parallel challenges facing a sales force and their efforts to amplify positive deviance. The outcomes, however, were highly divergent.

Neither was a minor initiative. Merck utilized PD to address below-quota sales of its blockbuster Fosamax across its sales force in Mexico. Goldman Sachs employed a methodology that mirrors PD to increase productivity of its three hundred wealth advisors distributed across the United States. Both initiatives were highly successful, documented by dramatic empirical increases in performance that have proven sustainable over time. Nevertheless, Merck has yet to utilize the process again. At Goldman Sachs, by way of contrast, the approach has been internalized as a way of running the business.

Does the success of the positive deviance approach at Goldman Sachs offer hope that the standard model is losing its grip on the corporate mindset? Probably not. Why? Goldman's Private Wealth Management division operates more like a loosely coupled community than a traditional company. Its wealth advisors are quasi-independent franchises, each with a set of loyal clients. (Perceived independence is important to providing impartial and objective financial advice to high-net-worth individuals.) Accordingly, upper management can't successfully "dictate" to these entrepreneurs. More analogous to the village stakeholders of Vietnam and Egypt, management recognizes that the best course is to shepherd intelligence and entrepreneurial energy in the ranks. Goldman Sachs adopted a strategy for herding foxes. Its unique adaptation of positive deviance fit the bill.

SIX

Girl Soldiers in Uganda

Reintegrating Outcasts

What happens when someone learns about positive deviance in a book and attempts to put it into practice? What are the common misconceptions and mistakes?

Jerry and Richard were to learn a great deal about this as their Land Rover negotiated the treacherous potholes on the dusty road to the teeming refugee camps of northern Uganda. Our host, Paska Aber, had gleaned what she could from a nutrition handbook that described the PD approach. Her "PD process" was already under way. Richard describes the midcourse correction that ensued.

THE ACHOLI PEOPLE OF UGANDA HAVE a tortured post-colonial history, having been on the wrong side of every regime change since the 1950s. Difficulty morphed into disaster when religious fanatics fomented rebellion in the late 1980s. The Lord's Resistance Army took initial aim at the hegemony of the central government. After years of meager military success, the rebels turned against their own. The ensuing devastation drove the entire tribe of nearly 2 million people from the countryside into the only marginally improved safety of refugee camps.[1]

Farming consumes about two-thirds of an adult's daily existence in Acholiland. This simple statistic conveys the disruptive effects of the LRA's reign. Driving farmers from the land deprives the population of its livelihood and the society of its identity. Today, unemployment stands at 80 percent. Learned helplessness is endemic and alcoholism rampant. A 2005 survey of the Pader District, ground zero for LRA atrocities, confirms the magnitude of trauma. Just under 70 percent of the camp's population had witnessed torture, 40 percent had witnessed killing, and 70 percent of women reported physical abuse. Close to half of all women (46 percent) had been raped. A sobering 63 percent of women have considered suicide.[2]

Squads of LRA pounce upon a sleeping homestead in the dead of night. They carry guns but use their bullets sparingly. Noise might alert distant neighbors and bullets are scarce. Silent but lethal is the sharp knife called a barong. Guerrillas kick in doors and brandish their weapons. A sleeping family is stunned into submission. Boys and girls big enough to serve the guerrillas as porters are torn out of the grip of pleading parents. A knife is used to puncture a hole through the skirt or trousers of each child. This simple expedient allows abductors to confine the children on a leash and drag them into the bush.

Armies live on their stomachs, and guerrillas are not spared this mundane necessity. Abducted children begin their indoctrination as porters, forced to cover large distances on bare feet, stand sentry, and for some, to eventually fight. Early on, the LRA experimented with captured adults. But grown-ups proved harder to manage and more wily in their ability to escape. Children are more easily subdued. A few kilometers into the bush and a ten-year-old has no idea where home is. Powerless, threatened, and periodically beaten, children come to identify with the aggressor—easy marks in bending to the doctrine of their new masters.

Initiation begins immediately. The day following capture, each child is forced to carry a ten- to fifteen-kilogram bag of salt or chickpeas.

Forced marches are typically ten kilometers cross-country to avoid conspicuous roads. Legs and feet swell, making escape impossible. Those who are too frail or drop their loads are executed. Fear and instinct for survival overrule all other considerations. Weaker children, particularly girls, become babysitters for officers' wives and are routinely passed around at night to lower-ranking soldiers as compliant sources of sexual gratification.

Some children are more durable than others. When psychological resilience is combined with an instinct for social dominance (expressed by bullying one's peers), an avenue opens beyond the brutal routine of a porter. Being a combatant brings higher status and a better lifestyle. To ensure recruits do not contemplate escape, guerrillas often accompany them back to their family homestead, where they conclude the rite of passage as a trainee by executing a parent, sibling, or neighbor. This irrevocably redefines the child as an outcast. The LRA becomes "family." Socialization is complete.

The child soldiers of Uganda have endured circumstances so dire as to defy human understanding. (See "Girls and Guns.") Abducted girls—traumatized by months or years of sex slavery and witness to other forms of unspeakable evil—escape to the "safety" of Uganda's refugee camps only to be shunned by their community and distrusted by their families. Saddled with one or more young infants (carrying the DNA of their former tormentors), they are left to fend for themselves with neither skills nor education. Tormented by nightmares and guilt, they are psychological orphans—excised chapters of tribal history that the wider community wishes to forget.

The point of these graphic vignettes is not to provide shock for its own sake or to prompt reader despondency. Rather, it is to establish the backdrop of searing hopelessness. And yet, against all odds, a few had found a way forward. As we shall see, the resilience of some positive deviant girls establishes a beachhead of hope for this community of outcasts.

Girls and Guns

It is a simple machine. Weighing only nine and a half pounds, costing less than a live chicken in some countries and dissembling into eight easily detached components, it functions in muddy, wet, sandy, and frozen conditions. Numbers speak to its ubiquity—100 million units in use—one for every fifty people on the planet. Its purpose? Killing other human beings. Attributed with a quarter of a million deaths a year (placed in context, this approaches the death toll of the 2004 Indian Ocean tsunami), this durable killing tool has been dubbed the poor man's weapon of mass destruction. One premillennium survey ranked the AK-47 among the top fifty inventions that changed the world—ahead of the birth control pill and Apple's Macintosh![a]

The weapon itself represents but half the calculus of evil. Commencing in the 1970s, cunning "leaders"—first in Cambodia, then Angola, Guatemala, Liberia, Sierra Leone, and the Balkans—began to combine the AK virus with a cheap, expendable, and highly reliable vector for delivery: children. Turns out girls and boys of ten or older are strong enough to carry a nine-pound weapon and disciplined enough to follow orders. They are easily resocialized. Induced to take amphetamines or cocaine to "make them invincible," they kill with the

Bringing PD from the Textbook to Real Life

Paska's broad face and ready smile belie the focus and determination of a human cruise missile. As noted, she and her team "knew" about positive deviance, having read the CORE PD/Hearth nutrition handbook from cover to cover.[3] The handbook wasn't "wrong" per se. Rather, it was misleading insofar as any field guide is not meant to be taken literally as a script. PD isn't a formal model or a ten-step process—it's more indifference of a gardener scything weeds. Children have become the weapon of choice in over fifty violent conflicts around the world.

Over three hundred thousand children are indentured to this dark calling (a dispersed infantry that would rank as the sixteenth-largest army of active personnel on earth). And when, as inevitably occurs, survivors escape, are injured, or follow a leader who abandons the cause, the outcasts became collateral damage.

One of the biggest hurdles on the road to full repatriation is redemption. It is what the girl soldier has done to others (as contrasted to the abuse inflicted on her by her tormentors) that tortures most. People have more power over their own capacity to forgive than influence over others who can offer or deny forgiveness. The coerced perpetrator carries psychic scars in memories of atrocities inflicted on others and is often engulfed by guilt. Saving one's own life by killing someone else deeply scars the psyche. In the kinship-centric culture of the Acholi, psychological destiny is largely determined by a calculus of compassion beyond the girls' control.

a. Larry Kahoner, "Weapons of Mass Destruction," *Washington Post*, November 26, 2006, B1; C. J. Chivers, "Russia's Trademark Gun, But Others Grab Profits," *New York Times*, July 15, 2007.

analogous to improvisational theater. It is paradoxically both spontaneous and disciplined.

The compelling "hook" of the PD idea is looking for those who succeed, focusing on the glass half full in a world of glasses half empty. In Uganda's camps, rife with resignation and fatalism toward the prospects of former girl soldiers, Paska needed little convincing to grasp PD's merits. She had invited us to "fine-tune" a process under way.

We listened and learned. Clearly Paska was accomplishing important work. Her team had provided counseling to the girls (allowing them to re-count their trauma again and again until the nightmares receded). Programs provided skills to source a new livelihood. But all of this bore faint resemblance to the positive deviance process described in previous chapters (aside from using the terminology). A good deal of *unlearning* would be necessary to grasp and apply the features that make the PD process unique.

We spent an enjoyable afternoon getting to know Paska and her team. We gradually assembled the jigsaw puzzle that captured Paska's approach and its many moving parts.

Good news. Paska had clearly established that exceptions existed—abducted girls who had acquired a core skill (e.g., catering) or obtained a microloan and were able to provide for themselves and their young child. The team had limited its focus to girls at risk. Given limited resources, Paska wanted to ensure that their efforts would encompass only single girls who (1) had one or more children, (2) had no parental or kinship support, and (3) had not completed a grade school education. Curiously, the criteria were intentionally broad so as to not limit the initiative to girl *soldiers* alone. The reason? Camps harbored considerable resentment against abducted girls. Investing scarce resources on these outcasts when other girls were vulnerable could exacerbate frictions. (These are the land mines that well-meaning outsiders frequently overlook.) All former girl soldiers *and* single mothers would be included in the process.

Paska outlined what seemed to be a successful change process. But, in contrast to positive deviance, it had relied on experts (i.e., Paska and her team) to identify the exceptional girls and their mentors (*wayas*) and de-code their practices. Their approach had also collapsed the distinct steps of the PD process (i.e., engage the community, define the problem, establish baseline conditions, document common practices, and discover PD strate-gies) into one. Finally, the workshops to disseminate "solutions" were both designed and taught by NGO trainers, not the community or the repatriated girls themselves. These are far from trivial differences. They highlight much of what separates the PD approach from the alternatives. Unless the community itself spearheads discovery, it doesn't own the "answers." Unless the community designs and staffs the workshops to practice the successful strategies, participants will not successfully "act their way into a new way of thinking," nor will the practices be sustainable. A penny drops. Paska's group begins to grasp, at least in concept, what is different about PD and why that difference is important.

Having taken stock of the good work now under way, our dilemma was whether to leave well enough alone. The team seemed earnest. They wanted to learn from us. So we singled out three areas in which their *textbook* understanding was at greatest variance with the essence of the PD process. These were (1) reframing problems, (2) facilitating group discussions in a way to mobilize action, and (3) ensuring the community does the heavy lifting in establishing common practices and discovering PDs.

Reframing Problems

In Uganda, as elsewhere, sponsors (e.g., the government of Vietnam, women's advocates in Egypt, hospital administrators in Pittsburgh, executives at Merck) are saddled with a problem they don't know how to solve. In Vietnam, this was malnutrition; in Egypt, FGM curtailment; in Pittsburgh, MRSA transmission; and at Merck, Fosamax sales in Mexico. The initial framing of the problem often turns out to be a placeholder. If experience teaches one lesson, it is that problem *reframing* usually occurs along the way. The surest way for a community to recognize a problem as its own is for people to frame it in their own words and ground it in their own reality. Stakeholders need to imprint on a problem as surely as a newborn colt on a mare.

Jerry broached the reframing idea with examples, such as the CEO of a hospital in Waterbury, Connecticut, who was worried about MRSA infections. The CEO defined the problem as "hand washing." "No," said the staff. "The real problem is communication." (Nonadherence to hand-washing protocols is but one example of poor communications with hospital administrators, patients, doctors, and nurses.) But "communication" is a very broad topic. So the group cast about for a concrete issue. They decided to tackle a worrisome statistic: 70 percent of patients don't follow or complete the course of treatment of their prescriptions. Now the problem was theirs. The group owned it. The PD process subsequently reduced noncompliance to 20 percent.

In Egypt, the problem was curtailment of genital cutting. However, women's advocacy groups had framed it as a public policy problem. They sought to identify PDs in their community who were better advocates with the media and more effective in lobbying government ministries. In effect, their view of the problem was "communication inadequacies" in shaping public opinion. But when the first group of village volunteers gathered at the monastery, they reframed the problem in entirely different terms: the problem for them was identifying mothers, husbands, and wives who had resisted genital cutting and getting them to share their stories.

"Overture in Jakarta" describes work with the transvestites, or *waria*, of Jakarta. As defined by the NGO sponsor, the problem was "to reduce HIV/AIDS infections within this at-risk community" by ensuring safe-sex practices between warias and their clients. His framing focused on PDs whose negotiating strategies with clients ensured condom use. But an afternoon with the transvestites themselves reframed the problem in a dramatically different way. For them the problem was lack of access to trusting and caring health providers and the general stigma associated with their identity as transvestites. The new focus was on PD clinics, doctors, and informal leaders in the transvestite community who managed to keep "girls" safe.

Jerry began the first "unlearning" session with a disarming question: "Given the objective of reintegrating abducted girls, what criteria might you use to select a specific PD topic?" Answers were broad and general: "An intractable problem where positive deviants have dealt with the problem with the same resources," Paska replied. "A widespread and important problem that exists in the community," offered Beatrice.

Overture in Jakarta

Waria (a compound of *wanita* and *pria*—the words for woman and man) is the Indonesian word for transvestites—men who are anatomically male but live and dress as women. Many earn their living as prostitutes and have alarmingly high HIV/AIDS infection rates. An international health organization wanted to try using PD to tackle this problem. They were quick to flag a major obstacle to the planned positive deviance workshop, however: "Your PD process works with *groups*—yet the waria work alone. Our only hope is to tackle the one-on-one relationship between the waria and the client."

Before embarking on any workshop, an essential first step is to meet with the community informally. This was especially important in strange new territory. It is difficult (indeed, almost reckless) to conduct a workshop without any sense for the people involved.

Yado, an attractive waria in her early forties, had arranged for a late-afternoon meeting with her peers. The tawdry setting, ferreted out by an incredulous taxi driver, was sequestered deep in a down-at-the-heels precinct of Jakarta. The gathering took place in a warren of seven rooms within a labyrinthine slum. Eighteen waria awaited. Over three hours, crammed together on the floor of the largest of the rooms in which this group lived, the challenge was to relate to their very different world. Our only agenda was to understand.

The waria talked about their lives ("very difficult"), their aspirations ("to find 'Mr. Right'"), and their fears ("dying of HIV/AIDS"—as many of their coworkers already had). Their lifestyle and occupation, so strange to us at first, began to recede into the background. Our separate life experiences were bridged by the yearnings common to all human beings.

Gloria launched into a humorous tale of how her "mami" had helped the previous night when she was hauled into the police station by a local cop. This triggered an obvious question: "What's a mami?" Mamis, we learned, were older, informal leaders of loose networks of waria. "There are eighteen mamis spread across Jakarta," Gloria explained.

In anticipation of the next day's workshop, other questions followed: "Are all mamis the same?" "Oh no!" came a quick response. "Three of the mamis are much better than the others!"

"How?" we asked.

"They take their role more seriously. For example, the best mamis insist that their girls use condoms." This practice, it turned out, was not common to most of the group nor was it advocated by most of the mamis. The exceptional mamis also insisted that their girls go to the clinic to test for sexually transmitted disease.

Nina, twenty-two years old and recently arrived from "her" home in the provinces, could not repress a protest: "I will *never* go to a clinic for testing again!"

"What happened?" we asked.

"Humiliation! I went in for my exam. The doctor asked me to take off my dress. When he discovered I had a penis, he blushed, made a rude joke, and rushed me out of the office." Other waria agreed that "doctors are dogs, and that's why we don't want to visit them." Another question: "So, all doctors in Jakarta are the same?" The answer: no. Two more-experienced waria cited three clinics in the city whose doctors were receptive and kind. For the majority of waria, however, visiting a clinic was an undertaking to be avoided at all costs.

The waria began to disperse to apply makeup and change into work clothes (short skirts, glittery tight tank tops that barely covered their silicone breasts) in preparation for the night ahead. A few hours of listening had made clear that the host NGO's framing of the problem in addressing HIV/AIDS risk reduction was too narrow. (The sponsor's insistence that we zoom in on superior positive deviant strategies for negotiating condom use between sex worker and client did not meet the pick-the-right-problem test.) More fruitful territory lay beyond the waria and their clients—with the exceptional mamis and compassionate doctors. Enlarging the inquiry to encompass all stakeholders produced a breakthrough: given better understanding of "the problem," this at-risk community (categorized as "too hard to work with") now beckoned as fertile ground for the PD process. The solution space had enlarged to suggest new pathways to curtailing HIV/ AIDS infection in the community's ranks.

The afternoon's conversation was only a prelude. A subsequent workshop engaged the waria in interviews with other waria, mamis, doctors, and clinic administrators. These documented the experience at most clinics (i.e., doctor disgust and embarrassment) and the laissez-faire attitude of most mamis. This in turn cast light on specific PD practices and set the stage for dissemination.

The serendipitous mention of mamis and clinic humiliation in our first meeting with the waria underscores why the PD process must necessarily evolve in an organic and iterative fashion, not in serial logic. Real life is circuitous; it does not unfold the way it's described in a book. The order of things varies; in this instance, the process had actually begun *before* the community opted into participation in an inquiry. (A routine "meet and greet" session shed light on much that was to follow.) Moral: the right next step at any given moment is shaped by group dynamics, not by the steps in the handbook. This first conversation saved us from pursuing the possible dead end of our sponsor's assumption that condom use with clients should be the focus of the effort. It is also worth noting that the inadvertent discovery of key stakeholders not initially recognized as relevant to the problem (i.e., mamis and doctors) came to light only because conversation with the waria was conducted in a uniquely PD fashion—open-ended and inquiring (as contrasted to facilitator led, preconceived, and solutions driven).

Jerry: "What if the solution to your problem is providing each girl with a sewing machine?"

Puzzled looks.

Paska: "It's more complicated than that. We have to change how they think about themselves, how they behave, their self-esteem. Otherwise they'll just sell the sewing machines to get money."

Ensuing discussion made the point that the PD process is necessary only when solutions require individual behavioral change and community social change. The approach is unnecessary when a technical remedy will suffice. PD is well suited for messy problems that have entangled root causes. There is no checklist or set of infallible criteria to pick the perfect issue. Just be alert to surrounding complications, we advised. We encouraged the group to select something important, but avoid problems that depend heavily on uncontrollable events such as a change in the national government.

Forget What You "Know" About Focus Groups

The second major topic for unlearning entailed misconceptions about facilitation, the objective of "group conversations" and how to conduct them. Schooled in social work and familiar with conventional field methods, Paska's team viewed all this as synonymous with "focus groups." Focus groups are commonplace in industrialized countries and were popularized by advertising agencies in the 1950s. Interviewers use prescripted questions to extract information. The "facilitator" in a focus group context adopts a comparatively narrow aperture of inquiry. Survey tools often include questionnaires with rating scales or yes/no responses.

Group conversations, as fostered by the PD process, are somewhere near the opposite end of a continuum. The term *group conversations* is chosen to signal that something very different is required. Certain kinds of questions help groups take ownership. Questions can be more transforming than answers. Powerful questions don't dig for information, but instead cause respondents to think. They evoke a choice for commitment and accountability.

The hardest part of facilitating a group conversation is serving as a catalyst—*not* as the leader. Picture a jazz combo that encompasses the facilitator and focus group participants. "Conversation" is the music. The PD facilitator is most definitely *not* the "conductor." Rather, each and every participant needs to riff off others' ideas—and anyone in the audience is welcome to join in and make music at any point. If everyone is looking at the "conductor," something is wrong!

Paska and her team ponder these principles. Chagrined glances. Paska explains the reason for their dismay. "After our previous focus groups we zoomed right in on potential PDs. We knew what we were looking for in advance. Some abducted girls had mentors (wayas), and they were doing better. So we got the names of these women and sought their help. We also observed that successful girls were more assertive and proactive, so we organized a workshop to teach them to speak up and say no, to resist trinkets and the promises of unscrupulous men."

Jerry highlights a final difference between plain vanilla focus groups and the PD approach. "When do you stop?" he inquires. Paska and her team answer in unison, "When you are no longer learning anything new. When you've covered all the different segments."

"Seems sensible, but that's incorrect," Jerry replies provocatively. "Group conversations aren't an extractive industry like bauxite or coal. They aim to generate conversation, to raise awareness and get people engaged. One hundred focus groups for a camp like this with eleven thousand people may seem like overkill (given the likelihood of encountering diminishing returns after the first dozen). But this assumes the conversations are about collecting information. In the PD process, the real objective isn't just 'knowledge' or getting an 80–20 understanding of the situation. The overriding objective is engagement, creating a buzz, mobilizing people to take action."

The mantra for the type of conversation sought is "never overreach." Overreaching happens when the listener leads the witness, puts words in people's mouths, and interjects his or her own agenda. Seemingly innocuous questions such as, "Is the problem x?" or "Do you think we can solve it by y?" err by shifting the locus of initiative to the facilitator (who is usually trying to get to the solution straightaway). Don't assume a high profile. The objective is to engage the *community* in a collaborative quest, not race to find the solution first. (See "The Elephant in the Room in East Java.")

Community Ownership: "Don't Do Something About Me Without Me"

The following day Paska and her team try their hand at facilitating group conversations. Three sessions proceed in parallel, each group clustered beneath the shade of ancient ironwood trees. They are self-conscious as they summon resolve to try to facilitate differently. The beehive hum of eleven thousand souls packed on a few hectares of trampled dust fills the air. Children play soccer with a makeshift wicker ball on an adjacent field.

The Elephant in the Room in East Java

In Indonesia, societal etiquette and parental shame conspired to enforce a code of silence with respect to a prolific industry—selling daughters to sex traffickers. A local NGO had observed a worrisome uptick in this market among the poor families of East Javan villages. One small region alone, Gadungsari, was exporting hundreds of young village girls to urban centers. Fear of exposure was compounded by concerns over violent repercussions for interrupting the supply channels of local procurers.

A low-profile positive deviance workshop was convened. Its ostensible purpose was to explore the "safe" problem of school dropout rates. Pak Kasmadi, the village leader, described how positive deviance works. As participants pondered various examples, applications to more sensitive social problems were introduced, such as reducing HIV/AIDS risk among sex workers in Jakarta and Burma and curtailing FGM in Egypt. These provocative illustrations prompted one outspoken volunteer to surface the issue of girls "going out"—a euphemism for trafficking. Oblique reference allowed a sliver of light to shine on a heretofore undiscussable topic. With encouragement from Pak Kasmadi, participants were soon sharing anecdotes on the tragic consequences of girls being "sent out" by their poverty-stricken parents.

Remarkably, the participants decided to give PD a try on this most untouchable of topics. They documented common practices. A mapping exercise, based on a door-to-door canvass, revealed that roughly 140 people were missing, of whom 78 percent were young girls fourteen to seventeen years old. Mapping also highlighted how the exodus was distributed among Gadungsari's twelve hamlets, indicating what level of influence was wielded by what trafficker. The group subsequently visited poor families that had resisted the temptation to send their girls away. Through the witness of positive exceptions, they gained confidence that something could indeed be done.

Fast-forward six months. Community watch groups had identified the homes of high-risk girls. Today, an early warning system dispatches volunteers to counsel the families of girls planning to leave the village. They introduce those at risk to positive deviant families who have addressed their economic shortfalls through other means (e.g., creating home gardens, consumption of fewer cigarettes). As an extension of the initiative, "big sisters" from the village stay in touch with girls in the brothels (by cell phones and prepaid cards) and provide counseling and avenues of escape. Local leaders, who had previously ignored regulations regarding submission of "travel papers," began to enforce them. The number of documented trafficking incidents has been reduced dramatically. The most reliable baseline survey showed thirty-three girls had left Gadungsari in 2004. That number was reduced to six in 2008 alone. The initiative was expanded in one hundred additional communities in East Java, encompassing five thousand families and 19,500 at-risk children.[a]

The hardest thing for trained field workers is believing in their hearts that ignorant, poor, uneducated people can have answers the trained people never dreamed of. Every field worker or facilitator carries internalized expectations about how we add value. Relinquishing the need to prove one's competence is difficult. Experts are "answers" looking for problems to solve. PD practitioners, on the other hand, are community mobilizers who catalyze others' empowerment. Group conversations are the means for translating these intentions into action. "Solving the problem" is secondary to tapping the distributed intelligence of the community to discover its own latent wisdom.

a. Arvind Singhal and Lucia Dura, "Protecting Children from Exploitation and Trafficking," monograph (Jakarta, Indonesia: Save the Children, 2009), 44–48.

A wizened woman glances curiously from her mud wattle hut. Her ramshackle door is held together by a galvanized skin of recycled oil tins. Still legible, the labels warn: "USAID. Not for Resale."

We zoom in on ebony faces set off smartly by bright gingham blouses and shawls. Facilitators bite their tongues and struggle not to fill the long, pregnant silences. Like the first few raindrops from a cloudy sky, someone finally offers an observation. Others join in. The conversation builds and flows in a dialect we cannot understand. Participation has begun. Ownership is taking root.

The conversations include abducted girls, teenagers in the camp with intact families, mothers, fathers, and grandmothers, and camp officials, who maintain a nondirective profile. This allows Paska and her team to witness how groups reframe problems in terms that most directly impact them. They discover that 30 percent of the abducted girls in camp had at least one unwanted pregnancy. (Many of the girl soldiers had become pregnant after being passed around to gratify guerrilla appetites.) Arriving in camp with a young child and no parents, they had no means of support. As "damaged goods," the girls were written off as unsuitable for marriage. By virtue of the LRA's initiation rites, which entailed (as previously noted) murdering a parent or other close relative, they were also estranged from their extended family (the Acholi "social security system" and foundation of personal identity). Socialized by their experience with the LRA to believe that "sex is the only thing we're good for," their initial relief in escaping to the camps was often followed by despair as girls reverted to transactional sex to make ends meet. The result was inevitably self-destructive. Their promiscuity was seen as inflaming repressed appetites of men, both young and old. The girls were ostracized. If a subsequent pregnancy ensued, the girl was caught in a downward spiral of desperation and dependency. How can they live out their lives? Will they ever rejoin the mainstream? What will keep them from becoming an underclass? A criminal element?

Conversations with diverse groups in the camp converge on "preventing unwanted pregnancies" as a meaningful and concrete problem.[4] Participants agree that the PD process will be an interesting way to tackle this.

Debriefing the following day, Jimmy, a quiet member of the team, speaks up for the first time. "Once I asked the question, 'So *no* girls in this camp are able to . . . ?'" he interjects, "it was like watching a lightbulb switch on. All from one simple question. The group seemed startled by their own response: 'Of course there were exceptions.' It was surprising how quickly the tone shifted and how readily they zoomed in on potential PDs." Jimmy had grasped how the somersault question transforms resignation into a quest for possibility.

"There was lots of engagement and debate," another member of Paska's team adds:

> But the girls were the slowest to speak up. Boys were more spontaneous and direct. Initially the discussion turned to easy explanations (e.g., laying the whole blame on crowded camp living). Valid, as far as it goes. Lots of discussion about the inescapable conditions of camp. Children sleep in small huts alongside parents. Proximity provides provocative tutorials as kids take in the sighs and silhouettes of sexual intercourse. Teenagers discussed how camp life had liberated them from their former homeland routines. Many could wander freely at night. The boys agreed that lack of structure fostered promiscuity.

Open-ended discussion leads to greater honesty and group introspection. Discomforting insights begin to surface. A statuesque woman with tightly braided locks and a shocking pink tank top volunteers that some adults in the camp are renting out formerly abducted girls. Apparently there is a brisk market among predatory neighbors. Many agree. Others add that girls are at risk even in school, from teachers and as "trophies of conquest" for gangs of boys.

One group clears a significant hurdle of mutual trust in surfacing the taboo topic of menstruation. Whereas the Acholi treat other aspects of sexual reproduction quite openly, this subject is wholly out of bounds. Abducted girls were universally deprived of the tribal source of counsel on these sensitive adolescent matters—grandmothers. Traditionally, girls sleep in their grandmother's hut in the homestead. This source of guidance was altogether missing in the camps, and many girls were abducted before menstruation had begun. If their first menstruation catches them unprepared and caught in a public place, shame, humiliation, and embarrassment ensue. These incidents are traumatic and the topic of whispers for weeks. They generate yet another stigma to overcome.

"The Acholi culture is comfortable talking about sex," Beatrice volunteers: "We have specific dances that celebrate a girl's coming of age. You participate in the courtship dances when you're ready. But discussing menstruation and early pregnancy isn't in our repertoire. Camp life disrupts the normal ways that grandmothers would educate girls about these things." Grandmothers aren't around to help with adolescent problems and impulses.

Experience has catalyzed an "aha" moment. Holding back as facilitators and avoiding leading questions has revealed two previously unidentified factors that impacted unwanted pregnancies: (1) an unspoken conspiracy within the camp to exploit the "lost girls," and (2) an unaddressed breach in preparation for a girl's coming of age—her relationship with her grandmother. The problem, initially confined to unwanted pregnancies among single mothers and girl soldiers, was now enlarged to encompass other stakeholders—camp leaders, sex brokers and exploitive parents, soldiers guarding the camps, schools, teachers, and grandmothers.

Results: Learning from the Positive Deviants

Paska and her team were poised to engage the community anew in identifying their positive deviants. Their practices held promise, and their eagerness was hard to restrain. This time they recognized that rushing forward to find "the answer" was a temptation they needed to resist. Like gift givers at Christmas, they needed to refrain from "opening the presents." It would be essential for the community to both discover and open the gifts for themselves—partly for ownership's sake, and partly because what they "discover" might be very different from what the facilitator thinks is in the package.

Over the course of the project, 190 vulnerable girls (of whom 40 percent had been abducted child soldiers) were enrolled in an initiative to eliminate unwanted pregnancies. At the onset, only 35 percent of the formerly abducted were cultivating agricultural products for consumption or sale. One year later, 73 percent of the girls were engaged in growing crops, and 47 percent had purchased domestic animals such as pigs, goats, and even cows.[5] Over a third had become vendors in markets. Ten percent were selling cell phones and prepaid phone cards. Over half reported savings of 50,000 shillings (about $31) after the first year. All scored over 90 percent in enhanced self-esteem, improved hygiene, and establishing a relationship with a role model among community leaders, mentors, and peers.[6]

"It's all in the 'how,'" Jimmy later observed. "It was *how* we facilitated the group that got to the *what*. *How* some of the likely PD girl soldiers went about getting access to sponsorship, seeds, and a little land, not just the *what* of their source of income."

Reflections

The greatest challenge for Paska and her team was moving from "field worker as problem solver and expert" to "field worker as catalyst."

Restraining their instincts as helper and expert required constant vigilance. Fieldworkers are often motivated by the value of our own expertise. Inevitably, we impose it on the organism we're trying to help. If, on the other hand, our premise is that the community already has the answers, the task becomes one of facilitating self discovery. Seemingly slow starts acquire astonishing velocity once a community takes ownership of its own problem and discovers its own proven remedy.

Instincts are central to the practice of many professions. The subtle tension between the expert and an organism's intrinsic gifts is illuminated by an analogy.

In the arcane world of concert grand pianos, there is an elite cadre of wizards. They are the technicians whose work extends to the subtlest, most sensitive aspect of piano care: voicing the instrument. Possessing an uncanny sense of sound, they can distinguish discrepant tones at micro levels. Their job is to tease the greatness out of every newly minted Steinway and Yamaha piano, and to enable instruments long in use to sing with synchronized luster in concert performances.[7]

Voicing a piano aims to optimize the composite chemistry of all elements—the bridge, ribs, sounding board, plate, strings, and myriad tiny moving parts, even factoring in the moisture content of the wooden case and levers and the felt of the hammers. Manipulating the tension of the strings for tuning, the positions of the moving members for ready response, and the felt of the hammers for sonority reveals the instrument at its best. The treble will be rich and round with clear projection. The bass will have resonant power. The action will be poised for intimate partnership with the player. Through mastery of these nuances and sensitivity to their nature, the wizard calls forth each piano's unique personality.

Each group conversation, like pianos, has its own unique personality. The challenge is to tease out all that each has to give. Trouble is, unlike a piano voicer, there are no strings to pull. The process is not mechanical; it's organic. The facilitator's role is to listen humbly and encourage this possibility to come forth.

You Don't Understand the Problem
Until You've Solved It

As witnessed in Uganda and elsewhere, the initial framing of a problem shifts as a community converges upon a concrete issue with tangible relevance. Supreme Court Justice Stewart Potter, upon reviewing an appellate ruling on sexual content, famously observed that while he could not define pornography, "he knew it when he saw it." His wisdom has relevance here. A curious thing about the framing of a problem is that it *always* changes when you engage the actual stakeholders. Second, you don't really understand the problem until you've developed the solution. It morphs into something else.

In Vietnam, the "problem" began as childhood malnutrition. As the inquiry got under way, a deeper problem arose—overcoming parental resistance to feeding children shrimps, crabs, and greens (viewed as unsuitable foods, analogous to feeding a child snails or earthworms in the United States or Europe). Further along, the "problem" morphed into altering ingrained traditions that governed when and how often infants were fed. So the villagers designed nutrition "workshops" leveraging social norms to alter caregiver feeding routines (e.g., collecting the supplemental ingredients each day, hand washing, feeding their children more frequently). PD problems are such that your understanding of what you're "solving for" is ever-evolving. Today's solution sheds light on a deeper layer of the problem in a forward spiral toward enduring remedies. "Solutions" have a shelf life. It's an ongoing quest.

SEVEN

Infant Mortality

The Way to Change a Community
(Is Not to Engage in Community Change)

*The Pashtun-speaking people in the remote mountains
of North-West Frontier Province, Pakistan, endure one
of the world's highest infant mortality rates. One of every
twenty newborns dies within the first year of life. A fiercely
independent people, their communities have a long history
of rebuffing the efforts of health authorities to address this
problem. Recognizing these inhibiting features as conditions
in which positive deviance often flourishes, Save the Children resolved to give the process a try. No prior experience
prepared the team for the formidable barriers they would
encounter. Monique describes a journey that combines the
overt intentions of saving newborn lives and the unintended
consequences of doing so.*

THE PASHTUN HAVE evolved an immune defense system
that has allowed them to keep the world at bay for the centuries since Genghis Khan. It is the cultural/anthropological equivalent of
the Great Wall of China—only far more enduring and effective. The topography of the region is the handmaiden of isolation. Tectonic forces have

splintered the earth into a labyrinth of mountains, canyons, steep-sided valleys, and inaccessible hollows. As this book goes to print, these highly independent tribes are a feature of the nightly news. Occupying the no man's land between Pakistan and Afghanistan, they belong to no nation and are governed via ancient codes of tribalism and honor. Some enclaves sequester Taliban, others Al Qaeda—and probably Osama bin Laden himself. In sum, here as among few spots on the planet one witnesses determined and steadfast isolation that has protected tradition for centuries. And this comprises the centerpiece of our tale.

When Save the Children (SC) was invited to pilot the use of PD to address neonatal mortality in the North-West Frontier, they made a strategic decision to choose difficult sites to demonstrate the power of the approach "against all odds." Monique was asked to advise local SC staff in what was regarded as a very risky venture. Garamthone and three other villages were the poster children of insularity, isolation, and suspicion of outsiders.

So how does one coax a community into tackling a problem it has never acknowledged as such? Most were aware that infant mortality was among the highest in all of Pakistan (85 deaths in every 1,000 births). Yet leaders and villagers were inured to all this as "Allah's will."

Explorations with village chiefs beforehand whetted the leaders' appetite to address the issue. Tantalized, the discussion turned to the challenge of involving the community. The first encounter with the villagers at large occurred on Thursday afternoon a week later. The village leader, joined by Mohammad Shafique, SC field officer in the region, broached the topic with a dozen men hunkered on low stools beneath the corrugated roof of a local tea shop. They were exchanging friendly banter around makeshift tables. After pleasantries, the leader asked if anyone was concerned about so many of their newborns dying. Silence. Then incredulity: "What do newborns have to do with us? Babies and childbirth are women's business!"

Prepared for such reactions through prior conversations with Shafique, the leader held steady and endured the inauspicious beginning. As tea was poured into and drained from cracked and stained glasses, he expanded on his concern with the bearded listeners. "Have any of you had a newborn die in your clan?" There was general agreement that many babies born in the village the previous year had died before they were two months old. The explanation: "Allah's will." But why had Allah singled out Garamthone? "Maybe it is time to look into this," the leader asked rhetorically. "Following prayers tomorrow, join me. Bring your friends." Pregnant silence. Imperceptible nodding of a few heads. One hand raised in acquiescence. Younger men, unconvinced, shrugged their shoulders and looked away.

The Invitation

The next evening found the tea shop packed with a surprising gathering of twenty. Following prayers and ritual acknowledgments, the leader put the group at ease with a Pashtun proverb. Then Shafique explained how PD had been used to address intractable problems in other communities. Using teacups as props (most empty, a few full), and gesturing toward the empty cups, he said: "Each cup is a household. How many lost their newborns within a few weeks of birth?" Then, pointing to the full cups, he asked: "How many infants survived? Would it be of interest to talk to the families of both to learn what's going on?" Conversation began. Over the following days the buzz resulted in a gathering in the square beside the mosque. More than a hundred men among Garamthone's three thousand villagers had trekked in from nearby valleys and farms. Several now-curious male activists spoke in favor of learning more.

Getting Baseline Data

It was agreed that a good initial step would be to create reliable maps of recent village experience with newborn survival. That very evening, the first of what was to become a number of such efforts took shape with improvised materials representing houses, streets, mosque, and market-place. Hunkered on the ground, using colored felt-tipped pens to code stones into categories (e.g., families with no children, families that had lost a newborn since the previous Ramadan, etc.), the men created an epidemiological map. A green dot on a village home denoted a newborn who had survived. Black denoted less fortunate households. Orange, yellow, brown, and purple indicated cause of death—umbilical cord infection, asphyxia, diarrhea, hypothermia, or extremely low birth weight. Participants became wholly engrossed. Sharing experiences engaged the men in a topic traditionally relegated to women. Reticence gave way to animated exchange. Why had some newborns, born under exactly the same conditions as those who died, survived and flourished? These conversations would ultimately pierce the shroud of "Allah's will."

Pashtun men and women live parallel lives. Women rarely leave the family compound and don't shop or handle money. Segregation of the sexes is total and it creates a deep chasm in life experiences. Communication between men and women in private is also very limited. If a Garamthone husband and wife discussed her condition during pregnancy, the husband would certainly conceal the fact from his male friends. Opprobrium, not admiration, would stalk the man who discussed "women's matters" or accompanied his wife to a prenatal examination.

Weeks later, the men of several hamlets decided that women should be allowed to participate in the process as well. They invited another SC staff member, Amama Ambreen, to convene a session with female volunteers. Fast-forward. Picture the women huddled closely together on a neighbor's bed, transfixed as Amama told stories of PD's success elsewhere. Her examples raised the possibility of addressing infant mortality. The women proved eager to engage. For many, this was the first time in their lives that anyone had solicited their opinions. The fact that Amama, an educated woman from Islamabad, would spend hours listening to them fueled self-confidence. Interest was as palpable as their accounts of losing newborns were heartbreaking.

As the men were compiling census data, a parallel endeavor unfolded among the women. In their case, beans were the artifact of choice for the mapping process. Analogous to the Eskimos' proverbial twenty-three words for "snow," Pashtun women traffic in the currency of beans, a staple of the everyday diet. Differences between beans are subtle to the untrained eye but as distinct as words in a dictionary for the literate. The women's maps had deeper texture. They understood precisely what went on in the first two to three weeks after each child was born. Considerable care was devoted to creating these epidemiological maps. They captured who was born, who died; babies that had diarrhea, were underweight, or experienced respiratory difficulties or umbilical cord infections but survived. The end result was a composite picture of the men's and women's efforts.

It was time to visit households. Preparation took several weeks. First, respective groups had to agree on how they would inquire about common practices. Next, they agreed to limit their focus to the interval beginning with the third trimester, extending through birth, and concluding with the first year of newborn life. Excluded from the inquiry were obstetric anomalies (i.e., breech births, premature births) and newborns with life-threatening birth defects. Over a period of weeks many separate groups were spawned of mothers, mothers-in-law, and traditional birth attendants. Later they would come together and share findings.

Reframing the Problem: From the *What* to the *How*

Unsurprisingly, the ensuing process was not conducted as "interviews" but informed through stories. Pashtun life is captured in oral tradition. While there are no written diaries or civic records, memories provide an astonishing wealth of detail. When a baby is born, neighboring women visit, discuss, observe, and commit to memory what happened and how. To accommodate this tradition, tactile objects such as homemade stuffed dolls were employed to capture what people *do*, not what they know. This impelled the classic shift from the "what" to the "how." Enactment confirmed that many households delivered the baby in an animal shed because delivery was regarded as messy. Some sessions evoked stoic accounts of tragedy as mothers-in-law, new mothers, and traditional birth attendants (*dais*) elaborated on infants that had turned blue and died a few hours after a winter delivery. Reenactment with rag dolls and crude material substituting for umbilical cord and placenta revealed how the dais' attention switches from the newborn to the mother as soon as the baby is born. Miriam, one of the oldest and most respected dais in the village, enacted the common practice of placing the naked newborn on the mud floor so those present could blow prayers over it. In the cold Haripur winter (with no source of heat or insulating blanket between baby and damp earth), hypothermia was the unintended result.

Searching for Positive Deviants

Once common practices had been captured, it was time for the PD inquiry itself—the search for PDs. Earlier mapping helped the group identify families who had "at risk" newborns who had survived against all odds. Small groups of male volunteers joined Shafique and his team to visit and chat with the male members of these families to find out what they had done. A similar process took place among the women. Pashtun tradition is exquisitely sensitive to *not* awarding social recognition to one person at the expense of others. It was understood that "heroes" would not be singled out—rather, discoveries would highlight successful practices, not individuals.

One mother-in-law mentioned using a *gadeya* (pillow). "Why?" the visitors asked. "Before the baby arrives," she answered, "I make a special pillow of rags to put on the floor and to cover the baby when it is born." "Show us," the visitors requested. She did. A member of the visiting team, a mother-in-law herself, interjected: "I do something similar. I immediately put the baby to the mother's breast and put a blanket on it."

The men's visits with male relatives shed light on the PD practice of using a clean razor blade to cut the umbilical cord. One PD husband had created a "clean delivery kit." Another took his wife to the clinic for a prenatal exam. The list of practical and successful expedients gradually expanded.

In parallel conversations, men and women discussed their findings. At times this triggered heated debate. Vetting ensured the most relevant strategies and practices would gain ascendance. Convergence wasn't always easy. A collision of opinions arose concerning the widespread custom of giving prelactate honey (*ghutti*) to the baby in lieu of its mother's milk. Conventionally, mothers delayed putting the baby to the breast for three days, relying on the ghutti instead. Yet almost all PD households violated this custom. Evidence that it endangered newborn lives was so compelling that adherence diminished by 45 percent within six months.[1]

Spreading a Benign Virus

It was time to share discoveries with the larger community. Separate male and female community meetings were carefully choreographed to share the findings from the home visits. Eager villagers came together to hear about some of the secrets that could save newborn lives. The design of this phase gave testimony to the villagers' latent creativity, confirming yet again that a community knows best how to engage its own. One women's team employed a grab bag. Onlookers reached in and pulled out an item (e.g., a makeshift pillow/gadeya) and had to guess its use. Team members would explain when the audience was stumped. The men's group created a "bazaar" with items displayed on a "shopkeeper's table." The audience selected "purchases" from an array of elixirs, creams, herbal remedies, religious articles, razor blades, scissors, and so forth. Participants explained the rationale for their purchase. This provided the conversation starter as to which items had actually been shown to save newborn lives.

One role play made a particularly strong impression. A used razor blade was moistened with a black felt-tipped pen, symbolizing infection. A volunteer was asked to cut through a green onion (the ersatz umbilical cord). Incision left the "infectious" color clinging to the severed onion. "Of course, we must use clean blades," counseled Safwat, a conservative elder in the group. "When we go to the barber, we insist that he change his razor before he touches us. Those who don't end up with infections or boils on our face. Men should buy a clean razor blade for the delivery," he concluded. "And we must insist that the midwife use them too." The simulation drove home what cautionary words could not. Three days later a newborn was seconds away from having its umbilical cord cut by the mother-in-law armed with a bamboo knife. A heated argument ensued as the assembled argued in favor of the clean blade purchased by the husband. The majority prevailed. Thereafter, most husbands took responsibility for buying clean new blades. A few created a "delivery kit" containing the blade and a clean piece of string to tie the cord.

Dissemination workshops tended to follow a trajectory. They led off with an introduction of technical PD practices (e.g., clean razor blades) but turned inevitably to the importance of the husband's involvement and support of his wife. One violated a cultural taboo by giving his pregnant wife special food (trespassing on the mother-in-law's authority). Then questions began: "What do you think of this?" "How about a husband taking his wife to the prenatal clinic?" "Where do you draw the line?"

At the conclusion of the community meetings, volunteers gathered together to develop a strategy to enable the whole community to practice the successful but sometimes controversial strategies that had resulted in newborn survival. It was decided that the men should gather once a month at the tea shop in their *mohallahs* (neighborhood meetings), recount stories of recent newborns, discuss what they should do, learn more about pregnancy and delivery, and perhaps practice some new behaviors. Women developed a similar plan for monthly mohallah sessions where more elaborate new behaviors were practiced as well as stories of deliveries where the new behaviors were adopted.[2]

Over the course of the PD journey, something unprecedented took place. Husbands and wives, through parallel discussions of infant survival, shared common experiences and interests. Husbands knew when wives were having their sessions, sometimes taking place in the fields where women worked. Had they learned something the men didn't know? A wife might greet her husband, wanting to know what his group had learned. She might be working on a skit for the workshop. He might be involved in creating the new "obstetric emergency fund." A strange new world: couples with common interests, women with valued ideas! Discussions between husbands and wives began spilling over into other areas as well—education, family expenses, village politics. For the first time in their marriage, some men and their wives became partners. An invisible bridge was beginning to span the chasm of gender.

Of course, the women were very careful not to breach any of the foundational taboos. They remained modest in dress and were careful not to be seen by men other than their husbands. Any responsibilities they assumed for the new infant survival activities were in addition to their traditionally assigned chores. In sum, in outward appearance, the immune defense response of the Pashtun culture encountered few overt provocations to mobilize the traditionalists.

Fast-forward six months. Garamthone's finale took ingenious form as a "Healthy Baby Fair." The day dawned hot and dry. At first light a group of men began setting mats on the ground under a huge tent. Microphones and amplifiers had been trucked in from a distant town, and a group of young men were busy setting up and testing them. After tent, mats, and audio system were in place, it was time to unveil the community's solution to its gender segregation: twenty meters of gauze curtain strung down the middle of the tent, a diaphanous partition separating the sexes. Over the next two hours, more than five hundred men and women, boys and girls sat under the same roof and listened to talks by dais and men's and women's team leaders, highlighting the successful mother and newborn care practices. Duplicate flip charts with colorful illustrations of PD behaviors were used for the respective audiences. Songs with mnemonic themes were performed to general amusement. Men gave public testimony to the precautionary advantages of accompanying wives to the clinic for prenatal examinations and immunizations.

The healthy baby contest focused on children in three age categories (under one year, between one and two, and two to three years old). Babies were weighed and nutritional status noted. Multiple awards brought many mothers, and in some cases fathers, to the podium to receive small prizes. The point, of course, was to reinforce the focus on the effect of PD practices and to highlight the importance of the participation of both mothers *and* fathers in the survival and well-being of their children.

Invisibly, without transplant rejection, the impenetrable wall between the lives of men and women had been replaced by a gauze curtain. Its symbolic presence maintained tradition. Permeability symbolized transition to a new order.

Reflections

Change doesn't happen easily, of course, and the Pashtun immune defenses were not altogether lulled into complacency. Indeed, one oversight in the design was failure to include a sufficient number of mothers-in-law, whose traditional role was marginalized by the new practices. A resentful minority among them voiced opposition. While many hailed the Healthy Baby Fair as a great success, others, particularly older women, were outraged. One grandmother voiced disapproval with rhetorical flourish: "This project has created vulgarity by involving the men and showing pictures of pregnant women and other private female matters. The baby show was vulgar. Private female issues were discussed in front of everyone on a loudspeaker."

For every voice raised in opposition, dozens defended and supported the changes that were taking place. Tangible results were decisive: a measurable decrease in infant deaths. With evidence that birth outcomes could be affected by others "just like me," social and cultural equilibrium was irrevocably disturbed. The twists and turns of such emergent transformations are, of course, unscripted and unknowable in advance. Community change is complex. It happens through an infinite number of seemingly inconsequential things, during unheralded moments and subtle shifts in behavior that we may catch only out of the corner of our eye. Developments regarded as footnotes turned out to define the entire plot—for example, more meaningful dialogue between husbands and wives and greater parity between the opinions of mothers and their mothers-in-law. Focusing on concrete activities and better outcomes allowed supporting behaviors, networks, and roles to evolve naturally and invisibly. Transformation occurred precisely because *it wasn't* the intended objective.

Garamthone is a story about the consolidation of change. It is also a story about the importance of conserving all that is possible and changing only that which is necessary. That is the way nature works. Never in evolutionary history has a species abruptly reinvented itself from head to tail. Mutations are incremental. Small successes beget further incremental adaptations. All this was evident in Garamthone. Specific practices identified as endangering newborn lives were contained within the vessel of a tightly knit social system. Role definition of the latter made progress on the former impossible—unless both evolved together. True of all human arrangements, information (in this case, the best ways to save newborn lives) has a social life. Only by changing the social context can you change how "information" is interpreted and internalized. The extremes of Pashtun tribal culture only made this correlation more clear. Institutionalization of learning inevitably reaches into and alters culture, norms, beliefs, and values.

EIGHT

Nature's Way

Invisible in Plain Sight

THIS BOOK MAKES NO CLAIM that the positive deviance process is the only, or indeed the best, approach for addressing intractable problems. To the contrary, our initial expectations following Vietnam were that its relevance was restricted and applications localized. Observing its ascendancy over two decades has left us a bit in awe. Popularization of the idea has been almost exclusively through word of mouth (save occasional mention in the media). There has been no marketing campaign, investment in branding, or orchestrated publicity. Launching a Web site and establishing the Positive Deviance Initiative at Tufts University, in Boston, was largely a defensive maneuver to cope with a growing flood of inquiries per month from around the world. (See the box "Virtual PD?" for some conjecture as to the future.)

Why the fuss? The simplest answer, given a world (and media) largely preoccupied with "what's wrong" and "what's missing," is that the counterintuitive emphasis on "what's working against all odds" is a breath of fresh air. The approach is a tonic for the change-weary. It distinguishes itself primarily by focusing attention on the variants that succeed against all odds. (While the process relies on bottom-up initiative, this is not a

Virtual PD?

What might lie beyond the horizon as applications of the positive deviance process continue to proliferate and surprise us? One provocative application might occur in the virtual domain. It seems improbable, given our considerable emphasis on building a community, unfreezing the social system in which problems are embedded, and changing behavior. As a general rule, the electronic medium constricts and degrades the essential senses of sight, smell, touch, and feel through which humans bond with each other.

Then there is Linux, perhaps the most significant innovation in social architecture of the twentieth century. With sublime efficiency, it taps the intelligence of the many in the service of a highly productive software development "factory." It is a business platform with no center. It synchronizes interactions, fosters cooperation, achieves high levels of reliability, yet strips performance controls to a minimum. "Positive deviants" routinely defy conventional programming wisdom, introducing a superior practice or strategy that addresses some gnarly software challenge. The Linux "community" serves as a virtual market for brilliant outliers. This marketplace puts a PD module to work and stress-tests its viability.[a]

The Linux model is compatible with the ideas presented here insofar as it explicitly embraces the social context. In this respect, the distinguishing feature of Linux is not technological but sociological. Eric S. Raymond, author of *The Cathedral and the Bazaar*, observes that Linux dispelled the assumption that complex software must be written by a coterie of programmers harnessed to the yoke of weekly milestones. Rather, Linux offers itself up to be casually hacked by huge numbers of volunteers coordinated through the Internet.[b] Why not chaos? Because coordination is achieved not autocratically but via peer review. Linux is the poster child for how programmers and idea workers can self-manage when equipped with the right social architecture to undertake large, multidisciplinary tasks. This works in paradoxical ways.

Linux gets people to be more productive by *not* trying to drive them to produce. Rather, it operates like *American Idol* (i.e., peer acknowledgment and the satisfaction of contributing winning solutions is the currency of success). The key to lasting networks is finding ways to help others be more successful. Reciprocity is what gives a network legs. The Linux mantra is: "You give more than you get."[c] (Note that this differs markedly from the tenets of the standard model, which relies on instrumental contracts and economic arbitrage, i.e., swapping desired behavior in exchange for rewards to those who comply.)

Linux's reputational game is won both by pioneering a successful new initiative *and* by cooperating with others. We've seen examples of this throughout this book. Pioneers in Linux's virtual idea-land share similarities with PDs. They move beyond the frontier of the known—but not too far away. Programmers are bees in a waggle dance. Darwinian selection decides which PD modules make the final cut. Linux redistributes power based on reciprocity, trust, and social arbitrage. Status is awarded on a meritocratic basis in proportion to contribution. Sounds a lot like PD.

Markets are superior to corporations in fueling and funding innovations because (1) the marginal utility of an idea is assessed on a level playing field based on its merits (not politics or the whims of authority), and (2) there is an absence of overweening coercion. But few communities and organizations operate like an open market. The PD approach attempts to unfreeze the chronic impediments to change by engaging the community from the bottom up and enabling members to vote in favor of the PD practices that make sense. Linux does the same thing in the virtual world. Social capital is generated in human networks through the currency of goodwill, norms of reciprocity, and trustworthiness.

a. Eric S. Raymond, *The Cathedral and the Bazaar* (Sebastopol, CA: O'Reilly, 1999), 15–16, 21–63. See also Robert D. Putnam, *Bowling Alone* (New York: Simon & Schuster, 2007), 19–23.
b. Raymond, *The Cathedral and the Bazaar*, 16–17.
c. Ibid., 81–99.

unique attribute. Other participative approaches tap into the same vector of influence.)

Another explanation is that PD is more than the additive combination of best practices (which capitalize on indigenous variations that work) with an overlay of participative methodology. It is multiplicative insofar as it is a powerful synthesis of the best of both traditions.

There is a third and deeper explanation, and it has been a consistent refrain touched on in every chapter: the PD process works within a social system in much the same way that evolutionary biology works in nature. It is radical across time but incremental in a moment of time. It is disruptive with respect to a narrowly targeted problem, yet overarchingly conservative. It leaves most of the genome intact, altering only those elements essential for successful adaptation.[1]

Modularized Tweaks Versus Wholesale Reinvention

This last point warrants elaboration. Nature is selective in the way it innovates. It evolves piecemeal. A mutation that alters the size of the brain cavity does not require a change to the arms, legs, and torso. Computers exploit this concept. You can upgrade the hard drive without having to reengineer the microprocessor, server, or user interface. Positive deviance exploits this evolutionary pattern of modularization.[2]

In contrast, most human attempts at change disregard this principle. Organizations default to the big bang approach with wholesale reorganizations and new strategic initiatives. The debate over health care reform in the United States is a case in point. A nationwide reinvention of the entire system has dominated the discourse. Nature's way would be different, addressing the need for adaptive change through many small experiments. States partnering with the federal government could test several plausible solutions: ending Cadillac programs in one state, eliminating the tax deduction in another, creating a multistate consortium to enable insurance companies to compete across state lines, coalescing individuals and small businesses into groups of sufficient diversity to spread actuarial insurance risks. Over time, possibly five to seven years, superior schemes would prevail. Unintended consequences would be identified and addressed while pilots would be small enough to make unpleasant surprises manageable.

Positive deviance modularizes in two important respects. First, it narrowly focuses on the specific itch the community wants to scratch. PD avoids grandiose aims such as eradicating poverty in Vietnamese villages, revolutionizing gender roles in Pakistan, or leveling the status hierarchy of hospitals. Second, each social entity is a module in its own right. Solutions are never exported wholesale. Each community, NGO, or business unit within a company is regarded as unique in its own way.

Reproduction and Variation

Positive deviance is predicated on diversity and variation. In nature, sexual reproduction serves this role. Natural selection favors a process that generates variety over one that generates too much continuity. Turns out, sex is best.[3] The alternative, parthenogenesis (a rare process by which a few plants, ants, and worms conceive offspring through self-introduced combinations of identical genetic material), yields offspring identical to their single parent. Analogous to cloning, it is extraordinarily efficient in generating lots of progeny with few "defects." The trouble is, cloning bets the house on "one size fits all." It is far less likely to generate variations that thrive in new niche environments. In an organizational context, best practices are comparable to cloning.

Chromosome combinations from parents with different DNA generate variety in offspring. Sexual reproduction is nature's risk-mitigation function: variety increases the odds that species will find a way to survive in the face of disease or abrupt changes in the environment. Nature runs a prolific but indifferent R&D lab. Mutations too far from the norm (usually as the result of too many big changes at once) are aborted.[4] As many as one-third of pregnancies spontaneously miscarry within weeks of fertilization because the embryo is too radical to survive.[5]

These two intersecting properties of selectivity and variety give nature its potency and the positive deviance process its power. Both are predicated on arrangements that cultivate variety in moderation. (That's why it is important to reach beyond the usual suspects in embarking on the PD process.) Less obvious, variation is exquisitely sensitive to local conditions. (We observed this in the work with Jakarta's transvestites, in sales practices at Genentech and Merck Mexico, and in the essential adaptations of the PD process to the time constraints of hospitals.) Small details in the organism's ecology matter a lot as to whether a variant (positive deviant) flourishes or fails. Sometimes a peripheral development out of the corner of the eye turns out to be the main point. All-purpose solutions lose out because small variations in a particular environment require parallel minor adaptations for a species to flourish within it. Large scale, top-down change programs or lockstep generic techniques such as reengineering or Six Sigma often experience high failure rates because they ignore these essential truths. The PD process doesn't. A novel solution is disseminated through an infinite number of small adjustments. That is the way of nature—and it works in villages, corporations, and communities of every kind.

Preserving Cultural DNA

Social systems are natural extensions of the human genome. From the natural science perspective, Homo sapiens (and other advanced species) evolved a social repertoire to outcompete rivals for the same resources. Approximately twelve thousand years ago, hunter-gatherers discovered it was easier to raise plants than endure the nomadic life of searching for them. Remaining in one place favored the domestication of animals. This led to larger permanent communities and gave rise to more evolved cultures, which necessitated mechanisms of governance.[6] Accordingly, social arrangements became an important determinant of ascendancy or extinction. What we call "culture" is the name given to these unique properties—the social DNA important to a community's success and worthy of preservation. Variation serves to modify cultural DNA as it does with genetic DNA. Successful species discard that which no longer serves and preserve the rest.

The positive deviance process pays attention to balancing variation and preservation. This was of decisive importance in the progress made in reducing infant mortality in Pakistan. First, it turns to the intact community, not to experts, authorities, or an infusion of external resources. Second, it embraces the social system as central to deep human learning. Biological cognition and social learning are not separate and distinct. The mantra of the PD process is to leave as much cultural DNA intact as possible.

Phases of Change and Four Laws of Nature

Throughout this book, each story begins with an intractable problem regarded as "just the way it is." Equilibrium conditions accepted that 63 percent of Vietnamese village children under three were malnourished; stunting was the norm in the Altiplano of Bolivia; nineteen thousand Americans would die each year of MRSA infections; and nearly half of all children in Misiones Province, Argentina, dropped out before completing sixth grade. In nature, as in these situations, equilibrium over the long haul is a precursor to failure, not just figuratively but literally.

There is a natural progression of change within evolutionary systems.[7] These are incorporated into the positive deviance approach:

Prolonged equilibrium is a precursor to death or stagnation: when a living system is in a state of equilibrium, it is less responsive to changes occurring around it (e.g., complacent, resigned, ignoring or suppressing successful variants). Change entails disturbing this equilibrium (e.g., in the PD context, questioning fatalistic assumptions that "this is just the way it is" perturbs the status quo).

Somewhere near the edge of chaos is a sweet spot. Movement toward (but not over) that edge is propelled by threat or galvanized by a compelling opportunity. The *invitation* at the onset of a PD process provides the group with a choice to move out of its comfort zone. The somersault question evokes turbulence by challenging orthodoxies and focuses attention on the counterintuitive successes of outliers. This opens minds to experimentation and innovation.

Self-organization, as witnessed in every example in this book, occurs when this perturbation takes place. New forms and solutions often emerge from the turmoil. The most dramatic examples of these two phenomena took place in Pittsburgh and Pakistan. Emergence within the VA hospital revealed itself as patients, orderlies, and nurses were empowered to challenge the hierarchy and remind doctors to wash their hands. In Pakistan it altered the relationships between wives and husbands.

It is an empirical fact that most of the world's cities live forever.[8] Corporations, on the other hand, live half as long as the average human being. The explanation has to do with the self-organizing and emergent nature of cities as contrasted with companies. True, cities may cycle between decline and ascendance. But the complex interplay between a city's heterogeneous elements fosters continuing variation and adaptation. Corporations, in the name of efficiency, suppress variation by "getting all the ducks in line." To optimize productivity, they evolve highly refined and internally consistent operating systems. Payoff results—as long as the music lasts. But in the face of nontraditional competitors or major environmental discontinuities, all that streamlining and reengineering limits diversity, suppresses self-organization by those closest to the disruptive change, and curtails a bottom-up emergent response to cope more effectively. We witnessed this at Genentech and Merck. Nothing fails like success. Overadaptive organizations become inflexible. Disruptive change leaves them as helpless as a beached whale.

Unintended consequences are an inescapable feature of life. Living systems do not follow a linear path. One can disturb them in a manner that approximates a desired outcome—but never fully direct them. Leveling the status hierarchy at the Pittsburgh VA, strengthening the partnership between teachers and parents in Argentina, and bridging the gender divide in Pakistan exemplify outcomes that extended well beyond those that were originally sought or foreseen.

The positive deviance process traverses through all four phases. A nonconforming variant experiences an equilibrium condition as unsatisfactory and expresses its emergent potential to ferret out a winning formula. Then comes the kickoff to the PD approach, which not only perturbs the community's orthodoxies (e.g., upsets equilibrium) by causing stakeholders to reconsider whether the "undesirable" is "inevitable"—it also mobilizes its members in search of the variant in its midst. They self-organize to ferret out common practices and exceptions to the rule that are outperforming the norm. Emergence of preexisting and (as in the case of the Pittsburgh VA) yet-to-be-discovered solutions can occur. Emergence yields unpredictable, sometimes truly astonishing ways forward. Innovation is accelerated near chaos and emergence invites unintended consequences.

Let's zoom in on the term *chaos*. It evokes all manner of unpalatable images—pandemics, the stock market crash of 1932, cataclysmic meteor showers, even the wrong party winning the presidential election.[9] But "chaos" is all in the eyes of the beholder. Events that evoke one man's coronary arrest stimulate another's adrenalin rush. When we strive to catalyze disequilibrium and surf its edge in the positive deviance process, the question is always how much is enough. The group is the wisest guide in determining the productive threshold near chaos where minds are open and learning occurs. Beyond the upper threshold lies chaos itself. Trespass this boundary and the group may disintegrate. Learning shuts down. (Note how the groups in Uganda and Indonesia tiptoed up to the sensitive topics of menstruation and girl trafficking.)

The potential for unintended consequences is ever-present when tampering with a living system. It played out for the good in Pakistan where a narrow quest to improve infant survival bridged the gender gap and increased communication between wives and husbands. At Merck and Genentech, unintended consequences manifested as the corporate immune defense response mobilized itself to thwart further inroads of consultative selling.

Unintended consequences get to the heart of why you never really understand an adaptive problem until you've solved it. Problems morph and "solutions" often point to deeper problems. In social life, as in nature, we are walking on a trampoline. Every inroad reconfigures the environment we tread on.

Minimalist Leadership

Understanding nature's way—modularization, selective variation, preservation of cultural and biological DNA, and the natural progression of change—has clear implications for those in positions of authority. It calls for nothing less than a role reversal in which experts become learners, teachers become students, and authority figures become catalysts for bottom-up change. This isn't easy. It requires leaders to set aside their egos and habitual identities (being the go-to guy, the decision maker who knows what to do). What, then, becomes of the leader?

Notwithstanding nature's minimalist approach, important work still remains to be done. Specifically, the new work includes four primary tasks: management of attention, mobilizing those below to engage in discovery, reinforcement to sustain the momentum of inquiry, and the application of means to track progress toward goals. Instead of the "CEO" (chief expert officer), the leader becomes the "CFO" (chief facilitation officer). The job is to guide the PD process as it unfolds. This is as radically different from the traditional model of leadership as the positive deviance process is from the standard model.

Leadership begins with framing the challenge in a compelling way so as to engage others in generating an alternative future. Next, the task is to catalyze a conversation, paying attention to the social architecture to reach beyond the usual suspects and ensure the group takes ownership of its quest. The hardest part is to listen, pay attention, trust the process and the "wisdom of crowds," and permit the emergent potential of the community to express itself. A weathered marble tablet in Xian, China, commemorates the wisdom of Taoist sage, Lao-Tzu. A loose translation "reflecting our Chinese guide's best efforts and author interpretation" captures the essence of leadership in the positive deviance context with eloquent simplicity:

Learn from the people
Plan with the people
Begin with what they have
Build on what they know
Of the best leaders
When the task is accomplished
The people all remark
We have done it ourselves

In Summary

Earlier chapters have highlighted a number of steps critical to the success of the positive deviance approach. These include:

- Introducing PD as a proven approach for addressing adaptive challenges.

- Focusing on what's working against all odds (the positive deviant) rather than on what's wrong/what's missing.

- Commencing the process with an authentic invitation in which community members can opt in or opt out.

- Encouraging the community to reframe the problem to ensure relevance, concreteness, and measurability.

- Engaging the broader community (beyond the usual suspects) to host group conversations during which common practices are established and, subsequently, PDs identified.

- Ensuring that the community takes ownership of a design to disseminate new discoveries through action learning. Practice trumps "knowing about" the many permutations on information transfer.

- Remaining ever vigilant to the propensity of sponsors, outside experts, and facilitators to hijack the process. Their only role is as co-conveners (with community leaders) and catalysts of the group conversation. Their contribution should be as a musician in a jazz combo, not as the conductor of an orchestra.

Basic Field Guide to the Positive Deviance (PD) Approach

Purpose of the Field Guide

This basic guide is intended to orient newcomers to the PD approach and provide the essential tools to get started. It includes a brief description of the guiding principles, methodology, and process that have made PD projects successful. It is recommended as a resource to enable facilitators and apprentices to quickly initiate the PD process using the four basic steps (the four D's: *define*, *determine*, *discover*, and *design*). These comprise an iterative road map for the process.

Its brevity and simplicity are meant to invite curious and intrepid implementers who face complex problems requiring behavioral and social change. It is suitable for those who seek solutions that exist today in their community and enables the practitioner to leverage those solutions for the benefit of all members of the community.

PD is best understood through action and is most effective through practice.

When to Use Positive Deviance

Positive deviance should be considered as a possible approach when a concrete problem meets the following criteria:

- The problem is not exclusively technical and requires behavioral or/and social change.

- The problem is "intractable"—other solutions haven't worked.

- Positive deviants are thought to exist.

- There is sponsorship and local leadership commitment to address the issue.

Guiding Principles of the PD Approach

Remember these basic principles when initiating the PD process in a community:

- The community must own the entire process.

- The community discovers existing uncommon, successful behaviors and strategies (PD inquiry).

- The community reflects on these existing solutions and adapts them to their circumstances.

- The community designs ways to *practice* and amplify successful behaviors and strategies.

- Community members witness that "someone just like me is succeeding against all odds with the same resources that are available to me" (social proof).

- PD emphasizes *practice* instead of knowledge—the "how" instead of the "what" or "why." The PD mantra is: "You are more likely to act your way into a new way of thinking than to think your way into a new way of acting." Remember the wisdom of the villagers in Vietnam.

- Involve everyone; go to improbable places and to unlikely people to find solutions.

- "Don't do anything about me without me."

- The community creates its own criteria for success and monitors progress.

Characteristics of the PD Process

The PD process promotes behavioral and social change because:

- It is generative (i.e., it is self-organizing and emergent).

- It is based on strengths and assets.

- It is not "expert" driven. Community members provide culturally appropriate expertise.

- It is embedded in the social context of the community.

The PD process:

- Combines relational and technical considerations.

- Leverages existing formal and informal networks.

- Generates new networks and bridges barriers created by gender, status, expertise, and so forth.

- Promotes further change by inviting the community to monitor its own progress.

- Makes the invisible visible (i.e., calls attention to the PDs and the community's own hidden wisdom).

- Enables the community to translate its discoveries into immediate actions.

Tips for PD Facilitators

Tap the expertise in the group (remember: the people in the community are the experts).

- Ensure the participants talk more than you do. Encourage them to exchange stories and information among themselves.

- Refrain from making suggestions or giving advice (unless *repeatedly asked*).

- Ask open-ended questions (e.g. what, how, what if?). (Avoid questions that elicit yes or no answers.)

- Don't try to exercise control; let the group guide the conversation.

- Invite participants to tell their stories or share their experiences about the issue at hand. Tap into emotions.

- Make the process personal and fun.

- Share relevant personal experience with participants to make them feel comfortable. Develop trust by admitting your own vulnerability.

- Let silence speak! (Pause for twenty seconds after asking a question. That's long enough to sing Happy Birthday!)

- Stay with the questions. Don't press for quick fixes. Insights often come when one is least expecting them.

- Support a climate where speaking the truth is OK, even when doing so may make the facilitator or a participant look foolish, confused, or unprepared.

- Believe that there will be enough time. "Go fast by going slow."

- Commit to learn, to be influenced, to be personally changed by the experience.

The Art of Asking Questions

For the most thoughtful and revealing responses, use open-ended questions that ask what, how, why, why now? Here are some examples of what you might ask or say in specific situations to facilitate or refocus discussions.

To spur continued reflection and thinking within the group, you might ask:

- To answer your question, let me ask a question.

- Can I ask you a question about your question?

- I have a question for you . . .

To generate more interactive discussion among the group:

- Who can answer this question?

- Who wants to answer this question?

- Who has any idea about this?

- How would anyone here answer this question?

To involve more stakeholders, ask:

- Whose problem is it?

- Who else should be involved?

- How might we involve them?

To uncover or identify PD individuals or groups:

- Are there any groups of individuals who have overcome (or prevented) the problem?

You can also use the somersault question:

- So if I understand correctly, nobody here is (or has achieved) X?

- So, there are no people in your community who have overcome this problem?

Once the group realizes that PDs actually exist in their own community, then follow up with some direct questions, such as:

- How can we learn from them?

- When is a good time to meet with them?

To discover PD behaviors and strategies, ask probing questions:

- You said that you did X; how were you able to do that?

- Most other people have had problems with X and Y; how have you been able to overcome them?

- Many people have explained to us how difficult it is to do X because of busy schedules, high costs, conflict with community customs or traditions, etc. I was wondering what you do to overcome these barriers or challenges encountered by others in your community?

- How are you able to overcome these common challenges and barriers?

- Can you show us how?

- What do you do when X problem happens or you are faced by the challenge of Y?

- Encourage participants to repeat what they've heard or understood to get more specificity: "So, if I understand correctly, you do X only during the day and you do not do Y at all during the day or night?

- Do you know other individuals like you?

To help define or target actions to be taken, ask:

- What are our next steps?

- Who is going to do what?

- What will it take to accomplish this?

To ask permission to make a suggestion:

- Can I make a suggestion?

- Would it be possible for . . . ?

- You are the experts, but would it make sense if . . . ?

Commitment of Leaders and Sponsors

Before the PD process can begin, the first step is to identify a sponsor as noted below. This leads to assembling those who might potentially be interested in tackling an intractable problem. To do this:

- Introduce the PD concept and approach to potential sponsors.

- Extend invitations for involvement beyond the "usual suspects."

- Once potential participants are assembled and the PD concept is described through examples, ask: "Does this make sense? If so, is there anyone here who would like to become involved?"

- It is essential that this initial orientation to PD authentically allows potential participants to opt in or opt out.

- Enroll a resource team of volunteers that is diverse and includes members of the community as well as local leaders.

- Allow the group to invent the forms of organization and work processes that best suit it.

- Invite others who are willing, and at times eager, to become involved. Each person is valuable to the process.

Basic steps:

Step 1. *Define* the problem and desired outcome.

Step 2. *Determine* common practices.

Step 3. *Discover* uncommon but successful behaviors and strategies through inquiry and observation.

Step 4. *Design* an action learning initiative based on the findings.

STEP 1: THE COMMUNITY DEFINES OR
REFRAMES THE PROBLEM BY:

- Involving members of the community in generating or reviewing data that measures the magnitude of the problem

- Articulating a preferred future that is different from the past

- Exploring the issues impacting the problem and current behavioral norms

- Listing common barriers and challenges related to the problem

- Identifying all stakeholders who should be involved

- Sharing the group's findings in a community-wide meeting

TOOLS OR ACTIVITIES FOR DEFINING THE PROBLEM:

- Creating or using baseline data (mapping, creating visual score-boards)

- Establishing a time-framed goal known and agreed on by all (e.g., eradicate childhood malnutrition in our community within two years)

STEP 2: THE COMMUNITY DETERMINES
COMMON PRACTICES BY:

- Conducting discussions with various groups in the community to learn about common practices and normative behaviors

- Using participatory learning and action (PLA) activities such as mapping, improvisation, Venn diagrams, and prioritizing

- Continuing "focus groups." Even if what you're learning is repetitive, involve as many members of the community as possible in the conversation

STEP 3: THE COMMUNITY DISCOVERS THE
PRESENCE OF POSITIVE DEVIANTS BY:

- Identifying individuals, families, or entities in the community who exhibit desired outcomes

- Establishing exclusion criteria. Select only those individuals or entities who face the same or worse challenges and barriers as others

- Conducting in-depth interviews and observations by the community and PD facilitator(s)

- Identifying uncommon practices that correlate with better outcomes (having established common practices in step 2)

- Vetting the results with the whole community

TOOLS OR ACTIVITIES TO IDENTIFY AND LEARN
ABOUT COMMON BEHAVIORS (STEP 2) AND IDENTIFY
BEHAVIORS AND STRATEGIES FROM POSITIVE
DEVIANTS (STEP 3):

- In-depth interviews

- On-site visits for structured observations

- Discovery and action dialogues; as described in chapter 4, these brainstorming sessions serve to surface new, untried ideas once a community has been mobilized to address intractable problems

- Community feedback sessions on PD findings (see www.positive deviance.org for examples of PD inquiry tools)

STEP 4: THE COMMUNITY DESIGNS AND DEVELOPS
ACTIVITIES TO EXPAND THE PD SOLUTIONS BY:

- Expanding the solution space by engaging multiple stakeholders in applying the discovered existing PD behaviors and strategies

- Starting small to demonstrate success

- Connecting people who haven't connected before

- Targeting the widest range of appropriate community members

- Creating opportunities to practice and "learn through doing" in a safe environment with peer support

- Using imaginative approaches to involve the community in the work (e.g., feeding workshops in Vietnam, Healthy Baby Fairs in Pakistan)

TOOLS OR ACTIVITIES FOR DESIGNING OPPORTUNITIES FOR
COMMUNITY MEMBERS TO PRACTICE THE DISCOVERED
BEHAVIORS AND STRATEGIES:

- Community meeting to share PD inquiry findings

- Creation of an action team involving the resource team and self-selected volunteers who have participated in the process

- Develop an action plan; pin down roles and responsibilities

The community measures, monitors, and evaluates the effectiveness of its initiatives based on the PD findings by:

- Developing a way to monitor progress of initiative (assess, analyze, and act on information)

- Making progress real by engaging the community in developing its own indicators to monitor progress (quantitative and qualitative indicators of behavioral and social change)

- Creating culturally appropriate ways to communicate the data to the community as a whole

- Evaluating initiatives at regular, frequent intervals

As the process evolves and has a successful impact on the problem, other communities and groups will hear about the process and may want to learn more. Suggestions for dissemination might include:

- Documenting, evaluating, and sharing results

- Honoring and amplifying the success stories by storytelling

- Creating a living university for other communities to discover how the PD process could help them solve the same problem

Useful Definitions for Practitioners

The *PD concept* is based on the observation that in every community or organization, there are a few individuals or groups who have found uncommon practices and behaviors that enable them to achieve better solutions to problems than their neighbors who face the same challenges and barriers.

The *PD approach* is grounded in the assumption that communities have assets or resources they haven't tapped. The PD process enables a community or organization to identify and amplify those practices and behaviors, measure outcomes, and share their successful strategies with others. The PD approach is used to bring about sustainable behavioral and social change by identifying solutions already existing in the system.

A *PD individual or group* demonstrates special or uncommon behaviors and strategies that enable the person or group to overcome a problem without special resources. However, a person is defined as a PD only in the context of a specific problem.

PD design or *methodology* consists of four basic steps (the four D's: *define*, *determine*, *discover*, and *design*). These comprise an iterative road map for the process.

PD inquiry refers to the stage in the process whereby the community seeks to discover demonstrably successful behaviors and strategies among its members.

PD process refers to the entire journey encompassing the skillful use of experiential learning methods and skilled facilitation applied to the four steps of the PD design. It results in community mobilization and ownership, discovery of existing solutions, and emergence of new solutions as a result of community initiatives.

———————————

The Positive Deviance Initiative (PDI) would love to hear about your project. Please send us the following information:

- Name of your organization

- Contact information

- Name of the project

- Location of the project

- Problem statement

- Project impact

- Population impacted by the project

- Special target group

- Any documentation that might be shared on our Web site (stories, videos, photos, reports, articles, etc.)

Send this information to contact@positivedeviance.org, or The Positive Deviance Initiative, Tufts University Friedman School of Nutrition Science and Policy, 150 Harrison Avenue, Room 135, Boston, MA 01742, USA.

The Positive Deviance Initiative greatly appreciates your participation in documenting the ways the PD approach is being implemented worldwide.

This guide was developed by the Positive Deviance Initiative. For more information, go to our Web site at www.positivedeviance.org.

Introduction

1. Pascale interview with Miguel Angel Pinedo-Vasques, December 10, 2009; he had been studying positive deviants in agriculture, whom he calls "exceptional expert farmers." See also Ketzel Levine, "Farming the Amazon with a Machete and Mulch," *Morning Edition*, National Public Radio, February 4, 2008.

2. Michael Kamber, "In Niger, Trees and Crops Turn Back the Desert," *New York Times*, February 11, 2007, A1 (New York Edition).

3. *800 million do not have enough to eat:* "Global Governance Initiative, Executive Summary," World Economic Forum, Davos, January 2009, 7–9. *3 million will die:* Seth Berkley, M.D., founder of the International AIDS Vaccine Initiative (IAVI), Commencement Address, Brown Medical School Commencement Convocation, May 26, 2003.

4. "Global Governance Initiative," 11–12.

5. E. Benjamin Skinner, *A Crime So Monstrous: Face-to-Face with Modern-Day Slavery* (New York: Free Press, 2008), 265.

6. Jon Gertner, "8th Annual Year in Ideas: Positive Deviance," *New York Times Magazine*, December 14, 2008, 68–69.

7. For an updated list of PD applications across the globe, see Projects, Positive Deviance Initiative Web site (www.positivedeviance.org). Data cited in this paragraph are as of March 2009.

8. The Positive Deviance Initiative, funded by the Rockefeller Foundation, was established in 2008. Its mission is to disseminate the concept of positive deviance around the globe and touch the lives of 15 million people by 2015. Means of doing so include: (1) developing demonstration projects to address a spectrum of intractable problems in communities and companies; (2) training field practictioners; (3) creating communities networks worldwide; and (4) incorporating the PD methodology as a staple in the community change toolkit of the curricula of graduate schools of health, business, nutrition, development, and behavioral psychology.

9. David Pyle and Tricia Tibbetts, *Assessment of Active Experiential Training on Program Expansion: Living University in Positive Deviance/Hearth Program in Vietnam, 2002*. Published by the Basic Support for Institutionalizing Child Survival Project (BASICS II) for the United States Agency for International Development, Arlington, VA, March 2003.

10. "CORE Benefit Survey: List of PD/Hearth Program Implementation Sites 5/4/04," 2007.

11. Katherine Ellingson, Nancy Iversen, Jerry M. Zuckerman, Dorothy Borton, Kay Lloyd, Pei-Jean Chang, John Stelling, Alex Kallen, Monique Sternin, Curt Lindberg, Jon C. Lloyd, Margaret Toth, and John A. Jernigan, "A Successful Multi-Center Intervention to Prevent Transmission of Methicillin-resistant *Staphylococcus aureus* (MRSA)," press release for the Positive Deviance MRSA Prevention Partnership, March 2009.

12. Estimates based on Monique Sternin's field notes, conversations with Mohammad Shafique and Amama Ambreen, Save the Children Field Staff, 2001–2004. Mortality and morbidity was not documented empirically by the community. Alternate statistics as follows: An increase from 44 to 62.5 percent of mothers who received two or more antenatal checkups; an increase from 22.3 to 48.1 percent in the number of men who arranged for emergency transport should their wives require it; an increase from 19 to 33 percent of people who used a clean blade to cut the umbilical cord during delivery. See Save the Children, *Positive Deviance: A Strength-Based Approach to Behavior Change and Social Mobilization*, 2005, http://www.positivedeviance.org/projects/Brief_PD_Pakistan.pdf, 2005.

13. Save the Children, *Final Project Document Under USDOL and Save the Children, Inc. Cooperative Agreement* (Washington, DC: Save the Children, January 20, 2006).

14. Ibid.

15. Bapak Minarto, Community Nutrition Department, Indonesian Ministry of Health, "ADB Nutrition Improvement Through Community Empowerment," presentation, 2009.

16. Pamela A. McCloud, Shahira Aly, and Sarah Goltz, *Promoting FGM Abandonment in Egypt: Introduction of Positive Deviance* (Washington, DC: Centre for Development and Population Activities, 2003), 5.

17. See Ronald A. Heifetz, *Leadership Without Easy Answers* (Cambridge, MA: Harvard University Press, 1995); and Ronald Heifetz, Alexander Grashow, and Marty Linsky, *The Practice of Adaptive Leadership* (Boston: Harvard Business Press, 2009).

18. Jerry Sternin, field notes from the Altiplano, Bolivia, 2002.

19. For details on magpies and robins, see "Health Risk, Ornithological," *Pharmaceutical Journal* 280, no. 7487 (February 2, 2008): 132; H. Prior, A. Schwarz, and O. Güntürkün, "Mirror-Induced Behavior in the Magpie (*Pica pica*): Evidence of Self-Recognition," *PLoS Biology* 6, no. 8 (2008): 202; Gisela Kaplan, *Australian Magpie: Biology and Behaviour of an Unusual Songbird* (Melbourne: CSIRO Publishing, 2004); Arie de Geus, "The Living Company," *Harvard Business Review*, March–April 1997, 51–59; and Bruce Bower, "Songbirds Show Signs of Recognizing Their Own Bodies in Mirror," *Science News* 174, no. 6 (September 13, 2008).

20. For a discussion of the standard model, see Thomas Petzinger Jr., *The New Pioneers* (New York: Simon & Schuster, 1999), 91–93; and Richard T. Pascale, Mark Milleman, and Linda Gioja, *Surfing the Edge of Chaos* (New York: Random House, 2000), 12–15.

Chapter Two

1. See Marian Zeitlin, Hossein Ghassemi, and Mohamed Mansour, *Positive Deviance in Child Nutrition with Emphasis on Psychosocial and Behavioral Aspects and Implications for Development* (Tokyo: United Nations University, 1990).

2. Monique Sternin, Jerry Sternin, and David Marsh, "Scaling Up a Poverty Alleviation and Nutrition Program in Vietnam," in *Scaling Up, Scaling Down: Overcoming Malnutrition in Developing Countries*, ed. Thomas J. Marchione (Amsterdam: Gordon and Breach Publishers, 1999), 105.

3. U. A. T. Mackintosh, D. R. Marsh, and D. G. Schroeder, "Sustained Positive Deviant Child Care Practices and Their Effects on Child Growth in Viet Nam," *Food and Nutrition Bulletin* 23, no. 4 (2002):16–25.

4. David Pyle and Tricia Tibbetts, *Assessment of Active, Experiential Training on Program Expansion: Living University in the Positive Deviance/Hearth Program in Vietnam, 2002* (Arlington, VA: Basic Support for Institutionalizing Child Survival Project (BASICS II) for the U.S. Agency for International Development, March 2003), 1.

5. Robert B. Cialdini, *Influence: The Psychology of Persuasion* (New York: Harper Collins, 1984), 57–69.

6. Ibid., 89.

7. Ibid., 70.

8. Ibid., 71.

9. Ibid., 75–76. See also Edgar Schein, "The Chinese Indoctrination Program for Prisoners of War: A Study of Attempted Brainwashing," *Psychiatry* 19 (1956): 149–172; Henry A. Segal, "Initial Psychiatric Findings of Recently Repatriated Prisoners of War," *American Journal of Psychiatry* 61 (1959): 358–363.

10. Notwithstanding this caveat, the work on malnutrition in Vietnam scaled to two hundred villages through the "Living University." The initiatives on MRSA piloted in three hospitals have scaled to forty.

Chapter Three

1. Alexia Lewnes, ed., *Changing a Harmful Social Convention: Female Genital Mutilation/Cutting* UNICEF, Innocenti Research Centre, 2005, 3; http://www.unicef-irc.org/publications/pdf/fgm_eng.pdf.

2. Fatma El-Zanaty, Enas Hussein, Gihan Shawky, et al., *Egypt Demographic and Health Survey 1995* (Calverton, MD: National Population Council, Egypt, and Macro International, Inc., 1996).

3. Assaad Ragui, "Genital Mutilation Abandonment Programme in Egypt: Evaluation Summary Report," *The Population Council*, April 24, 2008.

4. Jerome Bruner, *The Culture of Education* (Cambridge, MA: Harvard University Press, 1996).

5. See Keith J. Winstein, "Ability to Quit Smoking Is Affected by Friendship," *New York Times*, May 22, 2008, A22, A29, D6; Clive Thompson, "Is Happiness Catching?" *New York Times*, September 13, 2009, MM28 (New York edition); Nicholas Christakis and James Fowler, "The Collective Dynamics of Smoking in a Large Social Network," *New England Journal of Medicine* 358, no. 21 (May 22, 2008): 2249–2258.

6. James Surowiecki, *The Wisdom of Crowds* (New York: Doubleday, 2004), 43, 116; Thomas Gilovich, *How We Know What Isn't So* (New York: Free Press, 1999), 115; Peter Block, *Community: The Structure of Belonging* (San Francisco: Barrett-Koehler,

2008), 371–378; Robert B. Cialdini, *Influence: The Psychology of Persuasion* (New York: Harper Collins, 1984), 116.

    7. Cialdini, *Influence*, 114–115.

Chapter Four

    1. Primary funding for the PD MRSA Prevention Partnership came from the Robert Wood Johnson Foundation's Pioneer Portfolio, which supports innovative ideas that may lead to breakthrough improvements in the future of health and health care. The health care organizations in the Plexus PD MRSA Prevention Partnership are Albert Einstein Medical Center, Philadelphia, PA; Billings Clinic, Billings, MT; Franklin Square Hospital Center, Baltimore, MD; University of Louisville Hospital, Louisville, KY; The Johns Hopkins Hospital, Baltimore, MD; and VA Pittsburgh Healthcare System. On March 23, 2009, the Robert Wood Johnson Foundation and Plexus Institute announced results from an analysis conducted by a CDC team that documented reductions in MRSA incidence ranging from 26 to 62 percent at three of the participating hospitals—Albert Einstein, Billings, and University of Louisville. These participating hospitals had the electronic data necessary for the study. CDC's analysis was presented at a special late-breaking session during the Society for Healthcare Epidemiology of America's 19th Annual Scientific Meeting on March 21. The CDC team concluded that successful implementation of the multifaceted MRSA prevention program using PD resulted in significant MRSA reduction with sustained decreases demonstrated over time.

    2. E. Lesky, *The Vienna Medical School of the 19th Century* (Baltimore: The Johns Hopkins University Press, 1976), 184–186.

    3. There is wide variance in the scary statistics on the MRSA threat; the most reliable stem from a 2005 study by the Centers of Disease Control. See R. Monica Klevens et al., "Invasive Methicillin-Resistant *Staphylococcus Aureus* Infections in the United States," *Journal of the American Medical Association* 298, no. 15 (2007), 1763–1774. See also Mitchell J. Schwaber and Yehuda Carmeli, "Don't Forget the Bacterial Threat," *Wall Street Journal*, August 12, 2009, A15.

    4. "Invasion of the Killer Bugs: The MRSA Issue," *Emerging*, newsletter of the Plexus Institute, Winter 2006, 8.

    5. Ibid., 5.

    6. Arvind Singhal and Karen Greiner, "Do What You Can, with What You Have, Where You Are," Plexus Institute, *Deeper Learning* 1, no. 4 (2007).

    7. Richard T. Pascale and Anthony Athos, *The Art of Japanese Management* (New York: Simon & Schuster, 1980).

    8. For an excellent discussion of these issues, see Joseph M. Hall and M. Eric Johnson, "When Should a Process Be Art, Not Science?" *Harvard Business Review*, March 2009, 58–65.

    9. An interesting, but inexplicable statistic that emerged at all the beta sites save one was that between 30 and 35 percent of the staff who show up for the kickoff meeting return the following day to volunteer. We've never quite figured out the significance of the one-in-three yield ratio, but it repeated itself in thirteen of the fourteen facilities.

Chapter Five

1. Merck corporate Web site fact sheet, http://www.merck.com/about/New_Merck_Fact_Sheet_Nov_09.pdf, 2009 (data from 2007); Peter Fotus and Joy Miller, "Merck Profit Jumps as Sales Inch Up," *Wall Street Journal*, October 23, 2009, 34.

2. Bruce Patsner, "The Vioxx Settlement: Salvation or Sell-Out?" *Health Law Perspectives*, University of Houston Health Law and Policy Institute, February 26, 2008.

3. See Clayton M. Christensen and Michael E. Raynor, *The Innovator's Solution* (Boston, MA: Harvard Business School Press, 2003), 10–11.

4. Alfred North Whitehead, *An Introduction to Mathematics*, rev. ed. (New York: Oxford University Press, 1948), as cited in Robert B. Cialdini, *Influence: The Psychology of Persuasion* (New York: Harper Collins, 1984), 7.

5. Peter Block, *Community: The Structure of Belonging* (San Francisco: Barrett-Koehler, 2008), 74.

6. Pascale field notes on Goldman Sachs, Sales Force Effectiveness Initiative, September 13, 2003; March 2, 2004; May 11, 2004.

Chapter Six

1. See Elijah Dickens Mushemeza, "Issues of Violence in the Democratization Process of Uganda," *Africa Development* ZZVI, nos. 1 and 2 (2001); Kevin Ward, "The Armies of the Lord: Christianity, Rebels and the State in Northern Uganda, 1986–1999," *Journal of Religion in Africa* XXXI, no. 2 (2001); Aidan Southall, "Social Disorganization in Uganda: Before, During and After Amin," *The Journal of Modern African Studies* 18, no. 4 (1980): 627–656.

2. Arvind Singhal and Lucia Dura, "A Positive Deviance Approach to Child Protection," Final Report, University of Texas Sam Donaldson Center for Communication Studies. Social Justice and Publication Series, El Paso, TX, October 23, 2008.

3. CORE Group, "Positive Deviance/Hearth: A Resource Guide for Sustainably Rehabilitating Malnourished Children" (Washington, DC: CORE, February 2003).

4. It is always better if group members reframe the problem more specifically in the context of their own lives. The chosen issue may not be the most critical or difficult or life changing, but engaging something they care about gets the process off to a good start. Sometimes groups select a problem with too many moving parts. Time and energy can be lost (along with commitment).

5. Arvind Singhal and Lucia Dura, "Protecting Children from Exploitation and Trafficking," monograph (Jakarta, Indonesia: Save the Children, 2009), 39–43.

6. Ibid., 22.

7. Perri Knize, *The Voicer: Grand Obsession, A Piano Odyssey* (New York: Scribner, 2008), chapter 12; Constance E. Barrett, "Interview with Marc Wienert," Zenph Studios, http://zenph.com/mwienert.html, September 1, 2006.

Chapter Seven

1. Save the Children, *Positive Deviance: A Strength Based Approach to Behavior Change and Social Mobilization* (Islamabad, Pakistan: Saving Newborn Lives Initiative, 2005), 12.

2. Use of data was key. While statistics and testimony were important, mohallah sessions introduced a pictorial checklist. The predelivery to postpartum care cycle was mapped as forty separate behaviors—each documented for its efficacy in saving newborn lives.

Chapter Eight

1. For an excellent treatment of this topic see Ronald Heifetz, Alexander Grashow, and Marty Linsky, *The Practice of Adaptive Leadership* (Cambridge, MA: Harvard Business Press, 2009), 13–17. See also Marc W. Kirschner and John C. Gerhart, *The Plausibility of Life* (New Haven, CT: Yale University Press, 2005).

2. Ronald Heifetz, conversation with author, August 10, 2009.

3. Richard T. Pascale, Mark Milleman, and Linda Gioja, *Surfing the Edge of Chaos* (New York: Random House, 2000), 28–30.

4. Ibid., 29.

5. Heifetz, Grashow, and Linsky, *The Practice of Adaptive Leadership*, 15; see also Kirschner and Gerhart, *The Plausibility of Life*.

6. Jared Diamond, *Guns, Germs, and Steel* (New York: Norton, 1997).

7. Pascale, Milleman, and Gioja, *Surfing the Edge of Chaos*, 19–170.

8. Jane Jacobs, *The Death and Life of Great American Cities* (New York: Random House, 1961).

9. Pascale, Milleman, and Gioja, *Surfing the Edge of Chaos*, 61–65.

Three authors, braided strands, complementary talents intertwining across time. Our affiliation has shaped lives, contributed to marriages, and altered careers over the two decades of collaboration in this work.

Jerry Sternin began his profession in 1962 as a Peace Corps volunteer on the island of Mindanao, Philippines. There, on a narrow wooden bridge in the tiny village of Marawi, he met Richard Pascale, on active duty in the U.S. Navy. A lifelong relationship took root.

Jerry became Associate Peace Corps Director, Nepal, and Richard began his graduate education at Harvard Business School (HBS). When Jerry's overseas tour ended, Richard's introduction paved the way for his appointment as Counseling Dean at HBS. A man of many talents, Jerry left HBS four years later to devote himself to one of his many interests—cooking. He opened a restaurant, Chautara (Nepalese for resting place), in Pembroke, Massachusetts. Chautara was awarded a five star rating in the *Boston Globe*.

Jerry's association with Harvard altered the course of his life. There he met Monique, a French citizen in pursuit of her master's degree. They married, "honeymooned" on a Peace Corps directorship in Mauritania, and returned to Harvard in 1981 for Jerry's postgraduate work in Asian Studies with a concentration in Mandarin. In the course of study, they were introduced to a peripheral research distinction—*positive deviance*—a term used to categorize the outliers occasionally encountered in fieldwork (i.e., those who defy the norm and succeed when others are failing). At the time the construct inspired no particular epiphany. It was filed away in the cerebral cortex.

Richard, meanwhile, had received his doctorate from Harvard Business School and commenced life as a professor at Stanford's Graduate School of Business. His interests lay at the intersection of strategic intentions and the attendant requirement to mobilize individual and organizational change. By the late 1980s he had become a respected teacher and bestselling author. Expertise also attracted consulting assignments, one of them with John Browne, newly named head of British Petroleum's exploration division.

The Sternins, now with a young son, left Harvard and rotated through a series of Save the Children directorships in Bangladesh and the Philippines. In 1989, the NGO made an offer that was hard to refuse: open the first field office in Vietnam. First hurdle: the venture needed funding, but host sensitivities were such that the funds could not come from an American source. Richard, still consulting to BP, learned of the company's plans to conduct offshore seismic tests in Vietnam's territorial waters. He introduced the Sternins' work to John Browne. A seed grant of $250,000 was provided to underwrite the start-up. BP's support continued over the duration of the project.

The next hurdle surfaced shortly thereafter, in 1990. Scars of the "American War" (as it is known in Vietnam) were both physically and psychologically manifest. The Ministry of Health wished to focus on the widespread prevalence of childhood malnutrition in rural Vietnam. As described in chapter 2, the proposed collaboration with an all-too-recent enemy was not straightforward. Preliminary visits before embarking on the venture made clear that receptivity was tentative, access to the population limited, and the window during which the Sternins must prove themselves short. What followed was the first of many successes using the PD approach over the next thirty years.

The sage, the steward, and the scholar; intertwined lives with complementary talents, joined by a profound appreciation of the capacity of people to discover solutions for themselves.

Jerry Sternin (who died on December 11, 2008) combined deep wisdom with an uncanny ability to connect with people of all persuasions. Maestro of many PD workshops across the years, he was charismatic, funny, self-deprecating, and engaging. His warmth and understanding were transformational for the many he touched.

Monique has a master's degree from Paris University in American literature and civilization. In 1975, she traveled to India and Nepal and developed an interest in cross-cultural communication. After a teaching stint in Paris, she moved to the United States for graduate study, receiving a master's degree from Harvard School of Education in 1978. Monique brings rigor to fieldwork: she was the steward of the learning, translating artistic impulse into replicable process. What works? What doesn't? What empirical foundation must be laid to determine whether verifiable progress has been made? The antithesis of a sober empiricist, Monique has a remarkable capacity to blend into the community she serves, listen at their feet, and see the world through the eyes of those she works with. As a result of these latter sensibilities, the PD process "tail" has never wagged the change problem's "dog." PD is not a doctrine. It has evolved as a disciplined yet highly malleable methodology.

Richard, author, teacher, and consultant, has focused on the challenges of large-scale change. In the fieldwork described here, he played a background role, documenting the process and occasionally cofacilitating workshops. He observed the Sternins in action in Vietnam, Bangladesh, Indonesia, Myanmar, Uganda, Argentina, and the Pittsburgh VA hospital. His contributions extended to posing skeptical questions about the mysterious bits, in particular whether PD constituted anything distinctly new. He has been involved in efforts to apply PD in the private sector. Finally, as the most experienced writer on the team, Richard took the lead in editing his coauthors' narratives, developing explanatory material, and assembling the pieces into a coherent whole.